BOLÍVAR
and the
Independence of Spanish America

BY
J. B. TREND

Perennial Library
Harper & Row, Publishers, New York

for

M.C.N.M.

BOLIVAR AND THE INDEPENDENCE
OF SPANISH AMERICA

Printed in the United States of America.

This book was originally published in 1965 by The English Universities Press, Ltd., London, in their Teach Yourself History series edited by A. L. Rowse. It is here reprinted by arrangement.

First PERENNIAL LIBRARY edition published 1968 by Harper & Row, Publishers, Incorporated, 49 East 33rd Street, New York, N.Y. 10016.

Contents

Boundaries of States in 1825
Statute Miles
0 50 100 200 300
CARIBBEAN SEA
PACIFIC OCEAN
PANAMA
Santa Marta
Cartagena
Maracaibo
L. Maracaibo
Curaçao
Pto. Cabello
Caracas
Carabobo
Cumaná
Barcelona
Trinidad
Merida
Ocaña
Cucuta
Orinoco
Angostura (Ciudad Bolivar)
NEW GRANADA
Ind. 1812, 1819
VENEZUELA
Indep. 1811, from Colombia 1829
Medellin
Tunjá
Boyacá
Bogotá
Magdalena
Meta
COLOMBIA
1830
REPUBLIC OF COLOMBIA
1819—1830
Guaviare
Cali
Sa. Pacaraima
Branco
Negro
BRAZIL
Yapura
Amazon
Quito
Pichincha
ECUADOR
Ind. 1811, to Rep. of Colombia 1822, Ind. Rep. 1830
Guayaquil
Napo
Iquitos
Marañon
10°
5°
0°
80°
75°
70°
65°
George Philip & Son, Ltd.

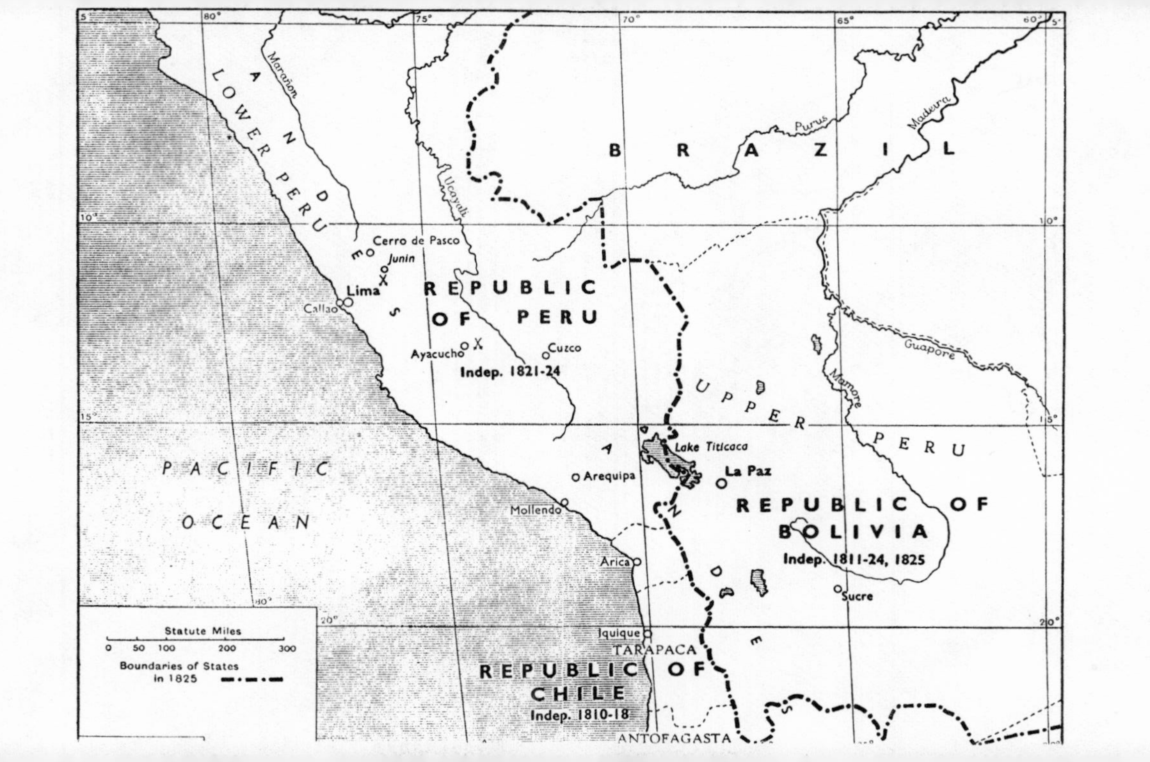
BRAZIL
Maraňon
Madeira
Purus
Ucayali
Guapore
Mamore
LOWER PERU
UPPER PERU
Cerro de Pasco
Junin
Lima
Callao
REPUBLIC OF PERU
Ayacucho
Cuzco
Indep. 1821-24
Lake Titicaca
La Paz
Arequipa
Mollendo
Arica
REPUBLIC OF BOLIVIA
Indep. 1811-24, 1825
Sucre
Iquique
TARAPACA
REPUBLIC OF CHILE
Indep. 1810-18
ANTOFAGASTA
PACIFIC OCEAN
Statute Miles
0 50 100 200 300
Boundaries of States in 1825

BOLÍVAR
and the
Independence of Spanish America

Preface

THE following study does not pretend to be based on new material. It is an account and an interpretation of Bolívar in the light of the large number of documents which have been printed since the last English biography was written in 1910. These documents include copious primary sources: the complete edition of the *Letters*, in ten volumes, by Vicente Lecuna (1929–30), the personal papers printed in the third volume of O'Leary's *Life* (suppressed until 1915), the original reports of the interview between Bolívar and San Martín at Guayaquil published by Carlos Villanueva (1913), and various other collections of diplomatic documents concerning Bolívar's foreign policy, notably F. J. Urrutia's *Páginas diplomáticas* (1917), and Sir Charles Webster's *Britain and the Independence of Latin America* (1938). Particulars of these, and other works, will be found in the Appendix.

I have tried particularly to bring out the importance of Bolívar's political theories, because they distinguish him from all other liberators. A chronological arrangement has been chosen; and though, by this method, military campaigns and romantic constitutions follow one another in an order which may well seem bewildering, an attempt to segregate political theory in one chapter, strategy and tactics in another and revolutionary politics in a third would have created an impression almost entirely fictitious. The thoughts and actions of Bolívar's life are only intelligible when taken together at the same time.

Most of the original materials are now in the Liberator's own country, Venezuela, and are preserved in Caracas in the National Library, the Academy of History, the *Museo Boliviano* and the *Casa Natal*: the house where Bolívar was born.

Chapter One

In the Spanish Colonies

IT could never be said of the Spaniards that they had conquered half the world in a fit of absence of mind. In that respect a Spanish colony was less like an English one than a colony of ancient Rome: part of a great and carefully planned policy of extending the rule, the way of life, the thought and the economic power of the mother country. But a Spanish colonist was hardly a free man. He was a dependant, under orders from the government at home, which appointed its own officials and allowed the colonist little say in the management of the country where he lived. So centralized a system gave Spain, as it gave Rome, a great advantage. While the British dependencies had to make their own way in the world, the Spanish dominions were from the first important achievements: Mexico and Peru were places of high consideration, famous all over the world.

The Spanish possessions in America were spread over a continent where distances are immense and communications most difficult. The rule of the Viceroy of Mexico extended far north of the modern Mexican border on the Rio Grande: it covered—or was supposed to cover—most of the present States of Florida, Texas, New Mexico, Arizona and California, and even stretched into Nevada, Utah and Colorado. For a time it included Louisiana; but the real limits of the Viceroy's authority were never determined and even the theoretical limits are still in doubt. From the prairies north of the Rio Grande and the dusty cactus-deserts to the south, it passed to the high valleys round Mexico City, between seven and eight thousand feet above the sea. It embraced the dry limestone peninsula of Yucatán, the narrow tropical isthmus of Tehuantepec and the hot countries of Central America beyond. The Viceroy of Mexico, or "New Spain," ruled over lands and peoples more extensive, if not more varied, than those of British India.

In tropical regions, the differences of climate depend less on the season of the year than on the height above the sea; and this is true not only of Mexico and Central America but also of Colombia and Venezuela, the two northernmost countries in South America. In Venezuela, the "Spanish Main," most people lived in the fertile valleys running parallel with the north-east coast between offshoots of the Andes. Caracas, the capital, lay about six miles inland from the tragic port of La Guaira, in a mild mountain climate of perpetual summer and ever-blossoming flowers. Farther to the south the land sloped down to the *Llanos*, the river-plains of the Orinoco: a hot, wet country where a half-wild race of cowboy *llaneros* kept half-wild cattle.

Next to Venezuela came New Granada—"The New Kingdom of Granada" it was officially called. Occupying the north-west corner of the continent, it had a coastline on the Pacific as well as on the Atlantic; but it was cut off from Venezuela by high Andes to the north and by trackless river-plains to the south-east. The main entrance to the country was the long, steep corridor of the River Magdalena which had to be laboriously ascended from its mouth near Barranquilla, or from the splendid, walled Caribbean seaport of Cartagena de Indias—the New Carthage of the Indies. After a journey of two or three weeks by boat and a ride across the mountains by horse or mule, the traveller at length reached Santa Fe de Bogotá, 8,560 feet above the sea, the proud, isolated, intellectual Spanish capital.

To the south of New Granada, beyond the inhospitable region of Pasto, lay the little mountainous country now known as Ecuador, because on the map it seems to be hung on the Equator. In viceregal days it was subject to New Granada; but it had once been a presidency of its own, the Presidency of Quito, named after the chilly, springlike, flowery capital, perched 9,500 feet above sea-level, at the foot of some of the highest volcanoes in the world. The nearest port, Guayaquil, is about 300 miles away.

Farther down the coast, a little north of Paita, Peru began. The modern capital, Lima, had been built by the Spaniards, with the port of Callao eight miles off on the barren sandy shore. The Peruvian Indians, being independent of overseas trade, had preferred their capital at Cuzco, 11,440 feet up in the Andes, but connected with other inland places by excellent roads built long before the Spaniards arrived. The proverbial wealth of Peru had come mostly from the modern Bolivia, an inland country east of the great high-lying lake of Titicaca; and at Potosí, 13,600 feet above the ocean, the Spaniards had found a mountain of silver ore which lasted well into the nineteenth century.

Chile, the next country along the Pacific coast, began with the nitrate deserts in the north and only ended with Cape Horn in the Antarctic. It was a long, narrow country, at some places barely a hundred miles broad, with its frontier running along the topmost ridges of the Andes and its coast stretching for nearly 3,000 miles along the Pacific. Half-way down was a well-watered, rather Mediterranean district of marvellous fertility. The valleys seemed an earthly paradise: one of them was called for that reason Valparaiso; while inland between the low coastal range and the high Andes was the capital, Santiago de Chile. In the south, the weather was perpetually cold and it hardly ever stopped raining; it was a land of lakes and forests, and in earlier days had been stoutly defended by Araucanian Indians.

Round the Horn and 1,500 miles up the Atlantic coast was the Rio de la Plata, the "River Plate," a brown, shallow estuary, 100 miles long and from 25 to 50 miles broad, leading into a land of boundless grassy plains: the *pampa*. It had been discovered in the sixteenth century but was afterwards abandoned for a hundred years or so; while the cattle and horses left behind to roam the *pampa* had increased and multiplied beyond all computation. Buenos Aires lay on the south side of the estuary; Montevideo on the northern bank, in Hudson's *Purple Land* of Uruguay; while a thousand miles from the River Plate, and on one of the widest rivers running into it, was Asunción, now the capital of the inland state of Paraguay.

The rest of the Atlantic coast, as far up as Guiana with a huge slice of the continent behind, belonged to the Portuguese. First a colony, then (from 1822 to 1889) an empire, it became an independent federal republic—the largest country in America, the most varied and the one which may one day be the richest of all the countries south of the Mexican border. But the traditions of Brazil have always been Portuguese and not Spanish, and it had little or nothing to do with the subject of the present study.

Spanish America, with its new Renaissance towns and its old Indian villages, its fabulous mines and immense plantations, speedily turned into a new Spain—a Spain refashioned and replanted in a continent of the most diverse climate, landscape, vegetation and human inhabitants. Colonial society, when it came to settle down after the conquest, fell into a number of distinct classes. First there were the Spanish. Spaniards held all the Government appointments, the higher ranks in the army and the higher preferments in the Church; religion and arms were, it was said, the foundations of Spanish rule. Spain was the only country with which commerce was possible; import and export trade were mainly in Spanish hands, while the smaller businesses were conducted by Peninsular Spaniards and natives of the Canary Isles.

Next in the social scale came the *Criollos*, "Creoles." They were men and women born in South America of pure, or practically pure, Spanish descent and were by inheritance, by acquisition, and by their own efforts and those of their slaves, the greatest producers of wealth in the Spanish dominions. They were great landowners, mine-owners and cattle-breeders; and in the towns most of the house-property was theirs as well. Their town houses were built in typical Spanish-colonial style, and those which have survived are a joy to behold. The Creoles were proud of their birth, proud of their achievement in the new countries which they had made, and they were not anxious to meet the Government officials who had been sent out from Spain.

There was, of course, no sense of equality at that time; but the rigid system of caste brought one advantage. It left a place—though a very humble one—for the Indian; and the fact that the Indians continued to exist under Spanish rule gave rise to large numbers of mixed-bloods or *mestizos*. In Colombia and Venezuela they were called *pardos*, "browns," and lived mainly as small tradesmen and artisans.

The remaining groups included the Negroes, freed men and slaves, who were either domestic servants or worked in the mines or on the plantations. In contrast to the Negroes who lived with the white man in town or country, the Indians lived on the margins of society or else formed exclusive societies of their own in remote villages.

The Spaniards had a sense of responsibility—of trusteeship, one might almost say—for their colonies. It was a sense that was legal rather than religious. In law, the Spanish possessions were not colonies of Spain, but integral, self-contained portions of the Spanish monarchy, the link connecting the dominions with the mother country being the Crown. They were held in fief by the Crown, in virtue of a bull of Pope Alexander VI (Alexander Borgia); and were governed not by the Council of Castille, but by the King and the Council of the Indies. From the legal point of view the Indians were vassals of the King of Castille, lent or "commended" to a third person, the *encomendero,* who in fact could exploit them more or less as he liked. The law benefited the Indians by considering them as minors—though they were minors who could never come of age; but the law was often a dead letter through neglect of the *encomendero*, and the cruelty of the overseer in his absence. This theoretical relationship between the Spanish dominions and the Crown of Castille has sometimes been regarded as a mere legal fiction; but at the time of the wars of independence it became a fact of immediate practical significance.

The most important of the Spanish dominions were Mexico and Peru; but they were no more representative of Spanish America as a whole than the great Caribbean islands of Santo Domingo and Cuba, or the countries on the northern or north-western coasts of South America: Venezuela, New Granada and Quito. In all of these the most striking feature, the most characteristic thing in Spanish colonization, the most reckless challenge to the overwhelming forces of nature, was the foundation of towns.

To some readers, a question of local government will seem curiously out of keeping with the romantic associations of the "Spanish main." Yet the beginnings of local government form one of the most living branches of South American history; for they tell us the conditions under which people actually lived, and how they set about dealing with those conditions. The first thing men needed on their arrival in the country was a settlement: houses grouped together so that they could be defended against attack by the Indians. But the Spanish settlements were not mere military posts; they were towns, with the organization which a town normally had in Spain and other parts of Europe at the time of the conquest.

In the English-speaking colonies in America, towns generally grew up where they were wanted, to meet the needs of the inhabitants; but in the Spanish-speaking colonies "the inhabitants grew up to meet the needs of the towns." The laws of the Indies laid down the forms to be observed when a new town was founded, and gave the colonists full instructions how to set about it. The Spanish colonial town was created consciously to a definite plan. In this, too, the Spaniards were following the Romans; for the plan of a new Spanish colonial town, wherever the lie of the land allowed it, was the rectangular pattern of a Roman camp, or the sort of camp which Ferdinand and Isabel had built during the siege of Granada, and had called Santa Fe. The streets were laid out at right angles, with a large central square, where the cathedral would be, the Law Courts (*Audiencia*), the Palace of the Inquisition and the principal Government offices. The town may have been founded by one man, or by a group; but the founders went about their business with the scientific detachment of military engineers building a fort, or a group of industrialists fixing the site of a factory. This was totally different from the way in which most English colonial towns grew up—at any place where people had found it convenient to meet together for trading. The Spanish founder selected a site; if possible he would choose one like a shallow, inverted saucer, so that the water from tropical rainstorms could drain away without damage. He pegged out the area of the big square (the *Plaza Mayor*), set up a mark to show that they were subjects of the King of Castille, drew the lines of the straight streets and settled the extent of the municipal boundaries. Then he distributed the land in lots among the settlers, "according to their merit, their capacity, or the size of their families." The founder next proceeded to appoint an *alcalde*,[1] mayor, or sometimes two, and from four to ten *regidores*, aldermen and councillors. Afterwards, they were elected either by the other councillors, or by a meeting of the most influential citizens. The town council was called the *ayuntamiento* or *cabildo*.

The part played by the municipalities in the Spanish colonies may have been exaggerated by some historians. They may have been, as an Argentine writer has described them, nothing but the shadows of the shadowy free councils of the mother country. But in earlier times, in

[1] Cortés, before he started on his great expedition, was *alcalde* of a small colonial town in Cuba.

Spain, the municipal councils were anything but shadows; and the colonies preserved them, even after they had disappeared in Spain and Spanish absolutism was most oppressive. But the council was an oligarchy, not a democratic body. There should be no illusion on that point. The councillors needed certain social qualifications: they could not be shopkeepers or traders. Then, in 1594, election was replaced by purchase and the councillor held office for life. Occasionally a life-councillor was appointed by the Crown, for meritorious service; and this happened to a certain Simón de Bolívar of Caracas, who was nominated by Philip II in the sixteenth century. Eventually the *cabildo* of Caracas came to consist of twelve Creole councillors by purchase and four honorary councillors nominated by the Spanish governor.

The independence of the councils in America surprised an agent of the French revolutionary government, M. Depons, who was in Caracas from 1801 to 1804. It was, he says, the high respect which the Spanish nation had for these municipal establishments which persuaded the conquerors of America that their new possessions ought necessarily to have *cabildos* and be allowed to maintain them. They only really came to life, however, when the Spanish governor died or the governorship fell vacant; for then the *cabildos* ruled the province until the new governor arrived.

In the period of emancipation from Spain the *cabildos* stood alone between the inhabitants and social chaos. Woodbine Parish, the first British consul-general in Buenos Aires after the declaration of independence, was quite clear in his mind on the value of these municipal corporations. "But for the *cabildos*," he says, "and the municipal institutions which still existed in most of the principal towns in the interior when the Spanish Government was broken up, I believe every semblance of a legitimate authority would have ceased." These institutions, he thought, were by far the best part of the colonial system implanted by Spain.

The municipalities of Spanish America preserved what little liberty the colonists had; but in most matters they took their orders from the Crown—that is to say, from the Council of the Indies sitting in Madrid. The result was that the majority learnt only to obey, and to obey the letter rather than the spirit. Anything like self-government was beyond their powers: a colonist could no more have a share in the government of a Spanish dominion than a layman could manage the affairs of the Roman Catholic Church. In a British colony, on the contrary, a man might have a considerable share in the management both of his town and of his church, and learn how both were governed. The unthinking, unquestioning obedience exacted by Spain was all very well so long as the parent

State remained great and powerful; but it provided no training for people to act for themselves, when the time came to be independent. So when the Crown to which they owed allegiance was seized by Napoleon and their connexion with Spain was broken, the colonists had only the most elementary ideas of what they could do, and the different communities were like ships without rudders. The first Spanish-American attempts at self-government were improvisations, because three hundred years of political bondage to an absolute monarchy had atrophied all capacity for administration.

Compared with the might and grandeur of the Spanish Empire the English colonies looked very modest indeed. They had been founded with the royal consent, but they existed (it was said) through the royal neglect. They had to make a virtue of necessity, and their necessity brought them a virtue which the careful Spanish control had squeezed out. The English colonies had to rely on themselves in everything they undertook, whether it concerned their State or their Church, and this gave them a political education which the Spanish colonists were never able to obtain.

It is untrue, therefore, to say that the Spanish people had no tradition of self-government; and it is also untrue that the Spanish Empire was mismanaged by being managed from Spain, three thousand miles away. What happened in

Spanish America was that colonial administration of Spanish officials was so thorough and painstaking and carefully controlled from Madrid that the traditional Spanish sense of local self-management was never given a chance.

Outwardly, the power and might of the Spanish Crown were visible everywhere. The Viceroy [1] was to all intents and purposes an absolute monarch, and lived with all the pomp required by his office. His rule was despotic, but it was often enlightened, and during the eighteenth century many improvements were made. The two viceroyalties, Mexico and Peru, were modified, regrouped and redistributed. Presidencies were added, and new captaincies-general. New administrative measures were introduced, and new classes of officials sent out to take charge of them. Spanish administration in America never stood still. "She complies, too, she submits, she watches times," Burke said of Spain, when pleading in England for conciliation with America.

Venezuela became a captaincy-general in 1777; from that time onward it was a political and judicial unit. From 1786 it had its own *Audiencia,* or High Court and Council, acting in the King's name, and using the Royal Seal. The Captain-

[1] The title and office of Viceroy is Spanish, and was first given to the representative of the King of Aragon in Sardinia in 1323. There were Spanish Viceroys in Majorca (1349), Sicily (1415) and Naples (1509), and also in Granada after the fall of the Moslem Kingdom. The first Viceroy in America was Columbus.

General presided, but he was in no sense a despot; and the prospect of a searching inquiry when he retired and returned to Spain reduced the range of his power considerably below that of the modern president of a South American republic. A further reform in 1786 raised Caracas to an *Intendencia*, an institution brought in by the Spanish Bourbon kings from eighteenth-century France. The *Intendente* (or *Superintendente*) was chiefly concerned with finance; but he came to hold a position in civil affairs not unlike that of a bishop in the Church: a kind of overseer, intermediate between the district officers and the highest authority in the land; while in Treasury business the *Intendente* could act without consulting the Captain-General.

The finances of the colonies had occupied the Bourbon governments of Spain ever since the earlier years of the eighteenth century. In 1728, a chartered company was founded under the Basque name of *La Guipuzcoana*; it did much for the development of Venezuela. Many of the old Creole families had shares in it, and found it a satisfactory form of investment: they got the whole of their capital back, several times over. The Company benefited both Spain and Venezuela, particularly in the export of cacao, and it transformed the Valley of Aragua and other Venezuelan districts into thickly cultivated areas of coffee, cacao, maize, indigo and cotton, while the Llanos of the Orinoco exported hides and cattle. Some old-fashioned landowners, fearing that the privileged position of the Company might damage the privileged position which they held themselves, opposed its efforts and, indeed, almost involved the country in a civil war on that account; but the Royal authorities were alert and limited the Company's powers by allowing other companies to be formed on the same lines. The *Guipuzcoana's* monopoly was ended in 1766, but the development of agriculture in Venezuela went on under the protection of new dispositions made by the able ministers of Charles III. The *Compañía Guipuzcoana* brought economic and financial improvement in Spanish America; but the growing ease and prosperity of the colony were partly due to the courage and enterprise of smugglers: chiefly English and Dutch. Smuggling was profitable for all concerned, for the Venezuelans as well as for the smugglers themselves: even the Spanish authorities in the colony winked at it. The colony had, in fact, achieved something like free trade.

Charges of oppression, rigidity and incompetence have often been brought against the Spanish regulation of South American trade. Perhaps the restrictions were felt more in the River Plate provinces than on the Spanish Main, and events in South American history, when observed from Buenos Aires, often have a very different appearance when regarded from other parts of the continent. The policy of commercial isolation—

or insulation—was not exclusively Spanish. Portugal, Holland and Britain all attempted at one time or another to use their predominance in sea-power to establish an exclusive trade in various parts of the world; and trade with other countries was excluded, not by differential tariffs but by absolute prohibitions. In the case of Spain, the restrictions maintained by the Spanish Government at home were real and vexatious. There was the restriction of trade with America to two or three Spanish ports from which neither Spain nor America could export or import what they wanted; there were the roundabout routes for legitimate trade which only led to more smuggling by routes which were shorter and more direct; there was the prohibition of cultivating vines and olives, because these could be grown in Europe, and of building factories in America, which did not exist in Spain; and lastly there were the trade barriers between one American dominion and another, which encouraged the feeling of political separatism. "A hermetically sealed empire," one Venezuelan writer has called it. Spain's economic policy towards the colonies might be absurd, but who was more harmed by it than Spain herself?

The *Guipuzcoana* and the activities of smugglers helped to bring about a change of another kind, neither economic nor administrative, but intellectual; and though (as recent research has shown) it would be quite untrue to say that the ideas and the Age of Reason reached Spanish America through the efforts of commercial travellers and *contrabandistas*, they brought something else beside merchandise—books and ideas; the movement of thought which came from Locke and Voltaire and the Encyclopædia and ended in the French Revolution. In the Spanish dominions the only group open-minded enough to accept liberal ideas from Britain and France, and eventually from the United States, was the group formed by the educated Creoles. Spaniards living in the colonies were unaffected. To that formidable array of officials, colonial education seemed an unnecessary and dangerous novelty, and the provisions made for it were surprisingly small. Down to 1591 there was only one elementary school in Caracas. Then Simón de Bolívar, the life-councillor appointed by Philip II, obtained permission to build—presumably at his own expense—a grammar school and a seminary for the training of priests. There were objections and difficulties; the buildings were not finished for seventy-three years. Permission to establish a university, applied for in 1697 and refused in 1700, was only granted in 1721; and then it might only teach the same subjects which were taught in the seminary: theology, canon law and Latin grammar.

The universities in the Spanish colonies were confronted by what were afterwards known in Spain as "the traditional obstacles." The result was that they produced little love of learning or spirit of inquiry. Education in literature and the arts was due to private tutors engaged by the old Creole families. Books were not easy to come by; customs officers and "familiars" of the Inquisition were on the watch for them, and even those which passed through the customs—lists of them have been published—did not always reach their destination. There were severe penalties on the sale or printing in Spanish America of books of any kind, even devotional books, without a licence from the Council of the Indies in Madrid.

Yet new books reached the colonies in considerable numbers. A French visitor to a Venezuelan house was shown a hollow beam in the roof, where the owner kept his Rousseau, his Raynal, and other books, out of sight of the authorities; and in Bogotá, New Granada, a clandestine translation of *The Rights of Man*, which scandalized the authorities, was found to have been s[illegible]rreptitiously printed on one of the few hand[illegible]ing presses which had somehow manag[illegible] the country. The enterprising [illegible] Nariño, one of the true [illegible] of Spanish American [illegible]ly punished for his o[illegible]

[illegible]oles there were pr[illegible] more reading than is generally believed, especially in New Granada.

There were also Creoles who had overcome the obstacles placed by the Spanish authorities on foreign travel, and who visited Spain, and even Italy and France. The Creoles were musical, too, particularly in Venezuela. The man who did most to encourage the performance of music, towards the end of the eighteenth century, was a connexion of the Bolívars of Caracas: Padre Sojo, a travelled and enlightened priest, who had been in Rome in the days of Clement XIV, and brought back (about 1770) a library of modern music and some wind instruments: flutes, oboes and horns. These were increased by the Emperor of Austria, in appreciation of the assistance given in Caracas to a scientific expedition which had been collecting animals and plants. Padre Sojo and his friends used to meet in a garden at Chacao, near Caracas, where (since 1785) there had been an experimental coffee plantation. Among the performers were a M. Blandin and his two daughters, who played and sang, and Don Esteban Palacios, an uncle of Simón Bolívar the Liberator, who seems to have played the violin. They played quartets under the orange trees: Pleyel, Mozart and Haydn—the latest modern music. On one occasion the famous traveller Baron von Humboldt was present. Sometimes they played in Caracas, at the house of another friend of the Bolívars—the Marqués de Ustáriz; and there was a musical "academy"—mainly a concert-society—which met in several of the larger Creole houses. The professional members coached the amateurs, one of the principal teachers being Cayetano Carreño, a member of a family of musicians which was afterwards to produce one of the greatest pianists who have ever lived, the Venezuelan Teresa Carreño. The first pianos reached Caracas (probably from London) in 1796.

Painting had not made so much progress as music; but literature had begun to form—as music had already done—an indispensable part of social intercourse. There had been readings in the great houses. One of those present was Andrés Bello, afterwards one of the foremost Spanish-speaking Americans of his time. His ode to the agriculture of the torrid zone is one of the few South American poems of South American nature; but it was written later, in foggy London lodgings, and Bello, when asked to recite in the old Creole houses of Caracas, would declaim neo-classic odes or translations from Horace and Virgil.

As the Age of Reason drew to a close, the younger members of the old families grew less interested in music and letters and more attracted to politics. They were caught by the fresh winds of freedom blowing from France, and by the practical freedom won by the United States. There was also a faint breath of freedom remaining in the ancient Spanish institutions of municipal autonomy; and these conditions do much to explain the sudden ardour of the Venezuelan patriots in attacking the very foundations of the political structure set up by their ancestors. The dominant impulse came from pure ideas; and the rebellion, when it broke out, was first and foremost a rebellion of educated Creoles. A great age was beginning, they felt; and they were passionately interested in the information which, in spite of all regulations, continued to reach them. Revolutionary ideas from France—and in South America even the *philosophes* seemed revolutionary—combined with the startling success of the United States, set them thinking of their own situation. England had lost the best part of an empire; would Spain be able to hold hers? Such thoughts drew their attention to the possibility of self-government, or even of independence, and reminded them of the few ancient liberties which their ancestors had brought with them from Spain to the New World. How else are we to account for the sudden passion of the Venezuelan colonists for attacking the very roots of the authority under which they had lived for so long? They were young, active and intelligent; they belonged to the best Creole families, and hardly realized that, in bringing liberty to their country, they and their friends would be the first and worst sufferers—would, in fact, lose everything, or at least lose their whole world in order to gain their own souls.

PANAMA
Caracas
VENEZUELA
Bogotá
COLOMBIA
GUIANA
Br.
D.
Fr.
Quito
ECUADOR
BRAZIL
PERU
Lima
BOLIVIA
La Paz
PARAGUAY
Asunción
Rio de Janeiro
CHILE
ARGENTINA
Santiago
Buenos Aires
URUGUAY
Montevideo
George Philip & Son, Ltd.

Chapter Two

Bolívar's Youth and Travels

SIMON BOLÍVAR came from a long line of colonial ancestors who had founded settlements, sown plantations, worked mines and performed the little public service allowed them by the Spanish Government.

The name Bolívar (or Bolíbar) is Basque; in English it might have been "Millbank" or "Millfield." The second half of the word appears in the typical Basque surname Ibarra. The family came originally from the Basque village of Bolívar in northern Spain, between San Sebastian and Bilbao, under the shadow of Mount Azcárate and not far from Guernica. Sometime in the eleventh century, Basque villagers defending their traditional rights and *fueros* fell out with their bishop. The bishop's men defeated them, and their leader, Gonzalo Pérez de Bolívar, was banished with all his household and their good were confiscated. Two centuries later the family returned to their native heath from the neighbouring village of Cenarruza.

In 1911 the village of Bolívar included a squat-towered church built like a fort and defended by a high wall. At the other end of the wide, empty square was a large, rambling house, the "Big House," Casa Bolívar Jáuregui, which (in the eighteenth century) had still been inhabited by a member of the original family. This was not the original dwelling, however; the last remains of that, the Torre Bolívar or Bolívar Tower, had come down in 1470. In the church, several stones in the pavement bore the old family shield on which the most notable object was a millstone. Several branches of the family could be found in the Basque provinces, all apparently descended from the original Bolívares de Cenarruza. The church of Sodupe, between Bilbao and Santander, contained a superb brass of a man in armour, with the inscription: Here lies the Magnificent Señor Pedro de Bolívar, Captain of the Royal Household of the Emperor Charles V, and of King Philip II his son, Kings of Spain and of Yngalaterra.[1] Another branch, Bolívar de Munguía, was represented by the late Ignacio Bolívar, the great entomologist, one of the devoted band of scientists of the Spanish intellectual renascence which followed the war with the United States in 1898. True to the tradition of the family, Ignacio Bolívar refused to accept the Falangist government of 1939 and, at the age of ninety, left Madrid for Mexico, where his son is doing valuable scientific research.

The first member of the family to cross the

[1] The claim of Philip II to be King of England was based on his marriage to Mary Tudor.

Atlantic was the Simón de Bolívar already mentioned in the first chapter. After spending thirty years on the island of Santo Domingo, he had gone to Venezuela in 1578 with a new governor, Don Diego de Osorio y Villegas, to whom he was distantly related. He was an official in the Treasury Department; and in 1589 the City Council of Caracas appointed him delegate for the province of Venezuela, sending him to Spain to lay their grievances before Philip II. There were twenty-seven items in the petition, most of them relating to economic questions: but one demand was for the re-establishment of "personal service" by the Indians, "because, if the inhabitants are deprived of the said personal service, they will cease to be converted to our holy catholic faith and return all too easily to their idolatries, heathenism, and ancient rites and ceremonies"—an economic question in a theological disguise. Another demand was that pearls should be allowed to circulate as legal tender along with coined money.

Philip II was impressed by Simón de Bolívar, or perhaps found him so importunate that he had to get rid of him. He rewarded him with honorary titles. They were not empty honours, however, for besides the appointment as life member of the Caracas City Council, he was promised a pension on his retirement, which took place in 1607. He died in 1616. A descendant of his, Luis de Bolívar y Rebolledo, was mayor of

Caracas towards the end of the seventeenth century, and paid out of his own pocket for the fortifications of the port of La Guaira. Juan de Bolívar y Martínez de Villegas was the founder of the town of San Luis de Cura in 1690, and also mayor of Caracas. As one of the largest landowners in the district, he became *Justicia Mayor* (Chief Magistrate) for the valley of Aragua and *Corregidor* (Regional Commissioner) for San Luis and San Mateo—the estate which Bolívar the Liberator afterwards regarded as his home, until it was destroyed in the wars of Liberation. This Juan de Bolívar y Villegas was his grandfather; his father, Juan Vicente de Bolívar y Ponte, added to his other occupations that of colonel in the militia. He died in 1786.

On his mother's side, Bolívar's family were equally distinguished; but to his mother herself, who must have been a remarkable woman, little attention has been given, for she died while Simón was still a boy. She belonged to one of the oldest Creole families, those *familias mantuanas*, which were called so because only white women of good family might wear the long mantle, or *mantua*—the name by which it was formerly known in England too. The Bolívars and all their near relations belonged to the *familias mantuanas*.[1]

Bolívar was born at Caracas on 24th July,

[1] *Mantua* is a Basque form of the Spanish word *Manta*, and it is tempting to connect the use of the word in Venezuela with the large number of old Creole families of Basque origin.

1783—the year in which England recognized the independence of the United States. He was christened Simón José Antonio de la Santísima Trinidad: and his surname—following the convenient Spanish custom which adds the name of one's mother after that of one's father—was Bolívar y Palacios. He was the fourth child, and had the misfortune to lose his parents in his childhood: his father at three and his mother at fifteen, but his guardians seem to have been kind and sympathetic. His nurse was a negress who had begun life as a slave and was called Hippolyta. "I never knew any father but her," Bolívar said. On one occasion, entering Caracas at the head of his troops, he saw her in the crowd: he left the procession, rode up to where she was standing and took her in his arms. There are several references to her in his letters, and among them is a letter dictated by Hippolyta herself. He saw that she had a pension.

The lively, imaginative and somewhat difficult little boy was not sent to school for long. There is no mention of the grammar-school founded by his ancestor in the time of Philip II; and the house in which the younger Simón went to school under the Licentiate Miguel José Sanz was in danger not long ago of being converted into a cabaret, had not attention been called to it in time. Private tutors were engaged, beginning with a priest and a Capuchin friar; and the young Bolívar was fortunate to have for tutor and companion Andrés Bello, then little more than Simón's own age, but one day to become (after living for twenty years in London) the greatest South American man of letters of his time, a considerable poet and the founder of modern Spanish grammar.

But the Liberator's chief tutor was Simón Rodríguez, one of the most original men and unorthodox teachers who could possibly have been found. His real name was Carreño—he was a great-uncle of Teresa Carreño the pianist—but he changed his name to Rodríguez through being involved (in 1797) in revolutionary activities against the Spaniards; while to intimate friends—and he had none more intimate than Bolívar—he was known as Robinson, after *Robinson Crusoe*. Before becoming tutor to Bolívar he had been appointed by the City Council of Caracas headmaster of a municipal school; but there, he had introduced a plan of "free" education which did not fit in with the ideas of the Spanish Government: he even brought in ragged children off the streets. Robinson lost his school, and left Caracas for Jamaica. Later, in London, he managed for a time to maintain himself by giving lessons in Spanish. In 1801 we find him at Bayonne, not far from the Spanish frontier of France, in company with an exclaustrated Mexican monk, Fray Servando Teresa de Mier, who had been persecuted by the clergy for a patriot, and forced to leave his own country. They went to Paris together and opened a school of Spanish in the Rue St. Honoré, their principal textbook being *Atala,* Chateaubriand's idyll of the Red Indians in Louisiana, translated literally into Spanish by Fray Servando but signed "S. Robinson, teacher of the Spanish language in Paris." One of the first to buy a copy was Chateaubriand himself.

At some time in his career Robinson married and had two children, giving them the names of plants from the French revolutionary calendar of Fabre d'Eglantine, which appointed days to trees, flowers, fruit and vegetables instead of saints. At that time Robinson is said to have been working in a chemical laboratory in Vienna. He never stayed anywhere for long. "I don't want to become like the trees," he would say; "take root in one place and never leave it. Wind, water, sun: everything that moves and never stays still. That's the life for me!"

In 1823 Bolívar, at the height of his success, heard that his old tutor, Robinson, had returned to South America. He wrote him an affectionate letter offering him ample support in his plans for a new system of education, and sent him to Chuquisaca in the south of Bolivia to try it out. The school soon had to be closed. Robinson complained that the authorities hindered his plans, or did not understand them; and when people saw him once more collecting poor children out of the streets and taking them into the schoolroom, some said that he needed the orphans to take him to heaven, while others declared that he intended to demoralize them so that they should go along with him to hell. "Only you understand," he protested to Bolívar, "because you see things as I do: that to make a new republic one must first make a new people." It is the old, old story of Spain and the Spanish-speaking countries: a new idea of education confronted by all the old traditional obstacles. Joaquín Costa and Francisco Giner were saying the same in Madrid eighty years afterwards.

With Bolívar for a pupil, Robinson adopted the educational method of Rousseau's *Émile*. Like Émile, the boy was rich, of good family and an orphan, and Robinson looked like the ideal teacher whom Rousseau had imagined. He devoted himself to the difficult problem of teaching the pupil practically nothing, in order that his mind might remain in the state of nature; but he kept a keen eye on the health of the boy's not very robust body. They lived mainly in the country, and Robinson developed in him that power of resistance and reserve of strength without which he would never have been able to withstand the physical hardship and mental strain of the long war of Liberation. A noted horseman, an intrepid swimmer, an untiring walker: even in later life few of his companions could compete with him. Yet Robinson had merely followed the recommendation of Rousseau, and by 13 the boy had little regular knowledge of anything out of a book. Rousseau would only allow one book for Émile: *Robinson Crusoe*; and though Simon Robinson's pupil read more widely than that, he was content with a general knowledge, derived mainly from poetry, history and philosophy. A few classical authors in French translations; Plutarch's *Lives*; a smattering of Locke and Spinoza; with Voltaire, Montesquieu, Rousseau, Volney, and other French writers of the Age of Reason—these were the sources from which the Liberator of the future acquired the elements of history, politics, religion and philosophy.

Later, he learnt to speak French fluently; and he read French poetry with such "facility, promptness and eloquence" that it might have been his own language he was reading. "I listened to him for more than an hour," his French aide-de-camp, Lacroix, said in 1828, "and only rarely did he ask me the meaning of a word." They were reading Parny's strange anticlerical poem *La guerre des dieux*. The writer most often mentioned in his letters is Rousseau, with Montesquieu a near second. Lower on the list, but equal in the number of references, are Plato and Las Casas, Homer and Horace, and Madame de Staël. But his favourite author was Voltaire. There he found everything that could be demanded: style and profundity, philosophy and fine criticism, and above all, wit: *diversión*. No great Spanish writer moved him, except Cervantes; he knew his *Don Quixote*, and returned in the last weeks of his life to the history of that ingenious but discredited liberator of a world of his own imagination. A Spanish writer of our own time, Unamuno, has claimed more than a touch of Don Quixote for Bolívar himself, while the men who followed him were all Sanchos. Even his manner of speaking was Quixotic; with a natural, unpremeditated emphasis that was very Spanish, though evidently influenced by the French writers of the end of the eighteenth century.

Bolívar's education did not end when he grew up. Even on active service he never let a day go by without reading; and as he made a habit of dictating letters, with a secretary to read reports and dispatches, he generally found time for reading for himself. He declared once in reply to a critic that though he had not read Aristotle, he was acquainted with Locke, Condillac, Buffon, D'Alembert, Helvétius, Montesquieu, Mably, Filangieri, Lalande, Rousseau, Voltaire, Rollin and Berthot, and in a box of books once forwarded to him were the *Iliad*, the *Odyssey*, Plutarch, Polybius, Cæsar, Hobbes, Grotius, La Fontaine, Ossian, *The Federalist* and Benjamin Constant.

When Bolívar's mother died his guardian (his uncle, Carlos Palacios) sent him to Spain. He was already an *alférez* (second lieutenant) in the militia of which his father had been colonel; and his slight boyish figure made him look, when in uniform, like Cherubino in Mozart's opera

Figaro. Embarking at La Guaira in a Spanish merchantman (1799), they touched at Vera Cruz on the Gulf of Mexico, where the ship was to load silver for Spain. The town was notoriously unhealthy; never, until modern times, was it entirely free from yellow fever. Bolívar profited by the occasion to ride up to Mexico City. He had letters of introduction to people in the official world; great ladies petted him and he was presented to the Spanish Viceroy. Like his hosts, the Viceroy enjoyed the company of the *caraqueñito* ("that boy from Caracas"), though he could not allow him to make indiscreet references to the "rights" of the Spanish American colonists to independence—which Bolívar is said to have done. Before the ship left Vera Cruz, the boy dispatched a hurried and ill-spelt letter to his uncle at home. They touched at Havana, whence they set out in convoy with another merchantman and two frigates, making the crossing in 27 days. A violent storm dispersed the convoy when it had just sighted Spain, and it was only after 13 days more of beating up and down the Spanish coast that the ship could make the port of Santona in the Bay of Biscay.

Once in Madrid, Bolívar went to live with his musical uncle Don Estéban Palacios. A great age of reform was just over, and things were beginning to slide downhill. The enlightened despot, Charles III—one of the few competent kings Spain has ever had—had died in 1788; and under his successor, the portly, priest-ridden cuckold, Charles IV, things had drifted back into the familiar waters of inefficiency, corruption and oppression, only relieved by the sprightly ladies painted by Goya: the *majas*, with or without their inimitable holiday costumes, and the *tonadilleras*, setting the Spanish fashion in music to the whole of Europe with the irresistible rhythm of their stylized popular songs. Bolívar, in Court dress, might have passed for one of the younger Bourbon princes in Goya's portrait-groups of the Royal Family; but the front of the stage was occupied by Charles IV's astonishing Queen, María Luisa, with her beautiful lace, and her ruined complexion; and by the slick, successful gigolo prime minister Godoy, known as the Prince of Peace. The Queen was amorous and prodigal of her favours. One of her chosen companions of the moment was a South American who had lived in Venezuela: Manuel de Mallo, a friend of Bolívar's uncle. The Queen used to visit Mallo in disguise, and on one of these occasions Bolívar had to escort her back to the palace in the dark. He was invited to come and play *pelota* at Aranjuez with the Prince of Asturias, afterwards the ill-natured Ferdinand VII. Bolívar liked to remember in later years, and to tell the story to the officers at his table, how he had hit the Prince of Asturias on the head with his heavy glove or racket. Ferdinand had made a fuss and complained; but his mother, who was watching, told him not to be a fool and go on with the game. "He little thought that one day I should pull the most precious jewel out of his crown," Bolívar said to General Mosquera.

The next thing that happened to Bolívar was that he fell violently in love. The lady was the daughter of Don Bernardo Rodríguez del Toro y Ascanio, second son of the second Marqués del Toro, who lived at Caracas. Don Bernardo agreed to the marriage, provided that the young people were prepared to wait; Bolívar was only seventeen and Teresa a little less. The Marqués de Ustáriz, who was acting as the boy's guardian in Madrid, was of the same opinion. He first persuaded Bolívar to sit down and do some work to improve his education, which, in spite of the efforts of Robinson, Andrés Bello and the two friars, seemed distinctly backward in Europe. The Marqués must have had a considerable share in forming Bolívar's mind at this time, and Bolívar always remembered it with gratitude. Then he was sent to Paris. His departure was hastened by an unfortunate affair in which he was stopped and searched at one of the gates of Madrid. The pretext was an order prohibiting the wearing of diamonds; but the real reason was that Bolívar was believed to be carrying love-letters between the Queen's favourite, Manuel Mallo, and another woman; and the Queen was jealous. Bolívar protested at being searched, and drew his sword on the police. The affair was hushed up, but he left for Bilbao (which happened to be the home of Teresa) as soon as possible and from Bilbao he went on to Paris.

He arrived there just after the Peace of Lunéville between France and Austria (9th February, 1801). Napoleon had become First Consul; victorious abroad, he was setting his house in order at home, and Bolívar was full of admiration. But on this, his first visit, his stay was short and his mind elsewhere. The ruins, material and moral, which had been caused by the Revolution were visible everywhere; and Paris did not make the great impression on him which it did when he returned in 1804. He hastened back to Madrid. The necessary formalities for the wedding were hurried through. An officer in the Militia, Bolívar had to obtain the royal consent; but by May 1802 all the preparations had been made, and Simón Bolívar y Palacios was duly married to María Teresa Rodríguez del Toro y Alaiza. They drove at once to Corunna, and took the next boat for La Guaira.

Bolívar had hoped to settle down on one of his estates by the side of his adored Teresa. He would be a rich man, and life on a plantation in the lovely valley of Aragua, varied by excursions to Caracas, held many attractive prospects. But Teresa died on the 22nd January, 1803, only ten months after they had settled down.

The death of Teresa was a staggering blow to

Bolívar. It was the crucial point in his career; it made him go back to Europe and turn his attention to politics.

> "I loved my wife," he said twenty-five years afterwards to Colonel Lacroix. "When she died I swore that I would never marry again and I have kept my word. If I had not lost her, my whole life might have been different. I should not have been General Bolívar or the Liberator, though I am quite sure that my temperament was never fitted to be *alcalde* of San Mateo. If it had not been for the death of my wife, I should never have made my second journey to Europe; and it is unlikely that, at Caracas or San Mateo, any of those ideas would have come to me which came to me on my travels."

Bolívar returned to Spain and landed at Cadiz at the end of 1803. He went straight up to Madrid to see his father-in-law. But in March 1804 all aliens were suddenly ordered to leave; the muddle and incompetence of Charles IV's government had led to a shortage of flour, and it was stated that there would not be enough bread in Madrid if the foreigners were allowed to stay there. Bolívar had to leave like the rest, and he went to Paris with his cousin Fernando del Toro.

Paris was a far more exciting place in 1804 than it had been in 1801; it had been enjoying itself in celebration of peace, victory and conquest. It was true that in the Place Louis XV, half hidden by a wooden hoarding, there still stood the scaffold which had seen the end of Louis XVI and Marie Antoinette. But these and other memories of the revolutionary past were dazzled by the present glory of Napoleon, while the unobtrusive return of the *émigrés* gave a sense of national unity which was, perhaps, deceptive. The *émigrés* wandered about a Paris which did not know them and which they hardly knew themselves. They seemed almost as strange as the foreigners who flocked to Paris from every country in Europe. Napoleon thought there were far too many from England, and by 1804 he was giving orders for them to be turned away. His autocratic rule was by this time so firmly established that the change from First Consul to Emperor seemed to many people little more than a change of title. It did not deceive Bolívar: it seemed to him the greatest disillusion of all time.

Yet the Paris of 1804, when the Consulate became the Empire, showed many outward signs of returning confidence. Trade was recovering, and the foreign visitors began to find something of the luxury and elegance of other days. The streets were still dirty and badly lighted; but they were a decided improvement upon Madrid or Caracas. On the Pont-Neuf gas-lamps were installed, "by which one could easily read one's newspaper twenty paces away." Then, as now, most Parisians lived in flats; but they had few comforts, and their furniture in the neo-classic style (*à la grecque*) had no easy chairs.

Shop-windows began to exhibit new and startling objects behind their small panes. The print-sellers' were full of grotesque, coloured caricatures, in the style of Rowlandson: caricatures of George IV, mixed with portraits of actors and musicians, and, of course, Napoleon himself. The more outrageous and satirical prints, with political implications, were sold surreptitiously. The streets were enlivened by signs, posters, caricatures. Carriages had begun to appear again; there were conveyances of all kinds: *wiskis*, *bogueys*, *demifortunes*, *cabriolets*, *fiacres*; pedestrians complained that they drove too fast. The street-cries were more piercing and persistent than ever: "Shoes to mend!", "Do you dream of cats?", "La belle Madeleine—cakes all hot!" Most insistent of all were the itinerant vendors of ink. Street-performers were everywhere: the *sorcier musicien*, playing four instruments at once, the "incombustible Spaniard" (a great sensation of 1804) drinking boiling oil and washing his hands and face in it.

One of Bolívar's favourite haunts was the Palais Royal. The galleries were illuminated by 180 gas-lamps; and under the arcades and out in the gardens were shops, cafés, restaurants, *cabinets de curiosités*, gaming-houses, money-lenders, *maisons d'amour*, and all sorts of curious types of humanity. A guide to Paris of the period (*Le conducteur de l'étranger à Paris*, 1812) warned the inexperienced that honour and virtue were banished from that spot; everything was lying in wait to entrap the unwary, though the wise would see there "the city of destruction and the palace of all the vices."

Bolívar inquired further. The centre of Parisian life was the Tuileries. A new court had come into being. The simple life of the First Consul and his wife at the Luxembourg had given way to a complicated etiquette; and when Napoleon or Joséphine needed a rest, and retired to Malmaison, even the parrots greeted them with cries of *Vive Bonaparte!* Lavish entertainment was provided. Talleyrand gave imposing receptions. But the highest point was reached by the assemblies of Mme Récamier, to which all Paris was invited: statesmen, generals, ambassadors, distinguished foreigners, men of letters and finance. Récamier himself was a banker, and Madame was *toute grace, toute vertu et toute bonté*—"one could not look at her without being in love with her, and one could be in love with her for ever for she never gave more than her friendship." It was the beginning of a great age of cafés and restaurants; many of the *restaurateurs* had formerly been chefs in great houses. Paris was the place where Bolívar could dine better—and with a more agreeable companion—than anywhere else in the world. The companion would be dressed in the latest *Empire* fashions, and memoirs of the time, such as the *Mémoires* of Madame de Rémusat, help us to imagine what these fashions must have been like.

The contrast presented to Bolívar by the "Palace of all the vices" must have been startling. He had been brought up on the pure eighteenth-century milk of the revolutionary gospel, which had been justified by the Revolution itself. France seemed then to a young foreigner, as Russia does to-day, the ideal country, the land of the millennium, where impossible political ideals had been realized and the most daring social theories put into practice; and this had produced a great, united nation for which countless citizens had been willing to sacrifice their lives because all had an equal stake in the country. That, at least, was how it looked from South America, and South America had got no farther than that. But coming from those remote parts to Paris, one was confronted by this extraordinary change of mood. The Revolution had failed after all, and had ended in Empire; its ideals had been compromised, and the new generation had lost the true revolutionary spirit and only wanted to have a good time.

Napoleon began the year 1804 by getting rid of undesirable English agents; then he set about having himself proclaimed Emperor of the French (18th May). The event was marked by three public ceremonies: on the 19th May he nominated fourteen Marshals of the Empire; on 14th July he awarded the first stars of the Legion of Honour; and on 2nd December in Notre Dame, the Pope, summoned from Rome for that purpose, administered the holy oil to Napoleon and Joséphine before the high altar. He blessed the ring, sword, mantle, orb, sceptre and crown. Napoleon took the crown and put it on his own head, then he crowned the Empress Joséphine kneeling before him.

Bolívar was disgusted, no less than Beethoven. Up to that time he had always admired Napoleon; but now, by becoming Emperor, Napoleon had become a traitor to his own ideals. Bolívar was unsparing in his criticism, both of the Emperor and of his supporters. He said as much in the presence of agents of the government, and made his hostess, Mme de Villars (his cousin Fanny Trobriand y Aristeguieta) anxious for his safety.

His disgust with Napoleon was distracted by the arrival in Paris of Alexander von Humboldt, the great traveller, just back from his celebrated journey to South and Central America. Bolívar was received by the great man, and spoke to him of the indignity of life in a colony and the great future of Spanish-speaking America when the Spanish colonies should be free. "Certainly, sir," Humboldt is said to have answered, "I believe that your country is ripe for emancipation; but who will be the man to undertake so vast an enterprise?" It had not yet occurred to Bolívar that the man might be himself. That idea came to him later, not in Paris but in Rome. But many years afterwards, in 1826, his cousin wrote, reminding him of the interview:

> "Baron de Humboldt is here . . . [but] I do not know what he means, calling himself a friend of yours. At that time [1804–5] when the success of your plan was still in doubt, he and M. Delpech were the most jealous of your detractors."

Humboldt was certainly wrong in telling Bolívar that the Spanish colonies had reached political maturity, and were ready for self-government. "If," O'Leary says in his *Memoirs*, "they had been ready for independence in 1804, many of the disasters which came afterwards during the revolution would have been avoided."

Jefferson, who was wiser even than Humboldt, was less indulgent to Spanish America, and said something to the effect that ignorance and fanaticism were incapable of self-government. He thought it better for the Spanish colonies to achieve their liberty gradually. Bonpland, the great botanist, was also wiser than Humboldt about Spanish American politics, and less pompous with Bolívar. He was friendly and encouraging, and assured the young man that a revolution always produced men worthy of it.

At this moment of doubt and hesitation Robinson suddenly appeared in Paris, and in March 1805 he and Bolívar set out for Italy. At Lyons they put their luggage on the diligence, and proceeded on foot through Savoy and Piedmont. They took eleven days to cross the Alps, stopping a week at Chambéry to see the house in which Rousseau had lived from 1738 to 1740 as the guest of Madame de Warens: the birthplace, it has been said, of the Supreme Being and of modern democracy, for both of those ideas were spread abroad by Rousseau. They reached Milan in time for Napoleon's great military review at Montechiaro near Castiglione. They stood at the foot of a small eminence from which the Emperor watched the march-past: Napoleon, Bolívar told Lacroix, looked at them carefully through a small telescope, and may have taken them for spies. Bolívar was greatly struck by the simplicity of the Emperor's dress, compared with the brilliant uniforms of his staff. It is doubtful whether he saw him put on the Iron Crown in Milan cathedral; but he seems to have remained there until after 8th June, when the two Venezuelans left for Venice. They made short stays in Verona, Vicenza and Padua, and perhaps reached Venice by the Brenta Canal and across the Lagoon from Fusina. Venice was rather a disappointment. From its name was derived the name of their own country, Venezuela; the lake dwellings of the Indians on the Lake of Maracaibo had seemed to the discoverers a little Venice. But so exaggerated an idea had they formed of the original, that in spite of the incomparable beauty of the city of the lagoons, and the glow of the sunlight which caressed the stones of Venice, the travellers were disenchanted and disappointed. One should see Venice before Venezuela!

They passed through Ferrara and Bologna and Florence, arriving in Rome at the end of June. The last few months in Paris had made Bolívar a new man; Rome moved him more than anything he had ever experienced. Years afterwards he tried to convey something of that first excitement to a friend in Venezuela. From his reading of Plutarch and Montesquieu and the inspiring conversation of Robinson, he saw in imagination the village of Romulus becoming the capital of the whole world. Here was a republican city-state which had conquered great empires, bringing their treasure in triumph to the Capitol and crowning with that offering the glory of the Senate. But his roseate view of Roman history was tempered by the consciousness of the mutability of fortune. That city, the marvel of republican virtue, home of the Gracchi, the Marcelli and the Scipios, was now a slave: the mere chattel of foreigners. What a theatre for profound reflexion!

Bolívar and Robinson lived at an inn on the Piazza di Spagna, near the great flight of steps leading to the Trinità de' Monti. It was the end of June and the weather was warm. Through Alexander von Humboldt, whose brother William was Prussian Minister to the Holy See, he met

Thorvaldsen, the Danish sculptor, and Madame de Staël, the contemporary best-seller who was just then collecting material for *Corinne*, a novel in which she saw herself crowned, like Petrarch, poet-laureate in the Capitol. The Spanish Ambassador procured a papal audience, but Bolívar declined to kiss the papal shoe with a cross fastened to the toe. The Ambassador was vexed and apologized for the disregard of etiquette, whereon Pius VII remarked "Let the young Indian do what he likes," and offered his hand. Bolívar kissed the ring with due reverence.

They explored Rome, sometimes driving, sometimes on foot. Bolívar had a strange passion for the Colosseum—not a very safe place in those days: for Rome, then and at other periods before or since, was full of doubtful characters from all parts of Italy, and the Colosseum was a paradise for pickpockets. One day they took a *calessino* and drove across Rome to the Aventine Hill. It was a hot afternoon, and Robinson remembered that they sweated copiously while they walked up to the top. On the side facing the Tiber the hill ends in a steep slope; from the other side they could see the tomb of Cæcilia Metella and the Appian Way leading out into the Roman Campagna. Madame de Staël compared it with the desert (which she had never seen), and thought Rome a mere oasis. To Bolívar, the sight of the Campagna brought a memory of the Campiña at home, round Caracas. They sat down "on a broken marble column" and began to talk of the Monte Sacro, where they were at that moment. This led to the subject of freedom from oppression: were they not on that very hilltop on which Rome had twice affirmed her inalienable right to freedom? Bolívar stood up, as though to look at the sunset, and delivered impromptu an impassioned oration on Roman history. Robinson's recollection of it was written forty years later, a tutor's reminiscence of a famous pupil's essay, which may be received with caution. Yet the style has a faint but indubitable echo of the *Méditations sur les ruines des empires* by the French Oriental traveller Volney, a book which Bolívar and several who came after him in Latin America —Sarmiento, Hérédia and Leconte de Lisle— all knew very well.

> "So this," he began, "is the city of Romulus and Numa, of the Gracchi and Horatii, of Augustus and Nero, of Cæsar and Brutus, of Tiberius and Trajan! Here all greatness had its pattern and all misery its cradle."

Octavius . . . Brutus . . . Anthony . . .Sulla . . . He went remorselessly through the list.

> "For one Cincinnatus there have been a hundred Caracallas, for one Trajan a hundred Caligulas, and for one Vespasian a hundred like Claudius. This city has indeed held gifts for all: severity for the ancient peoples, austerity for the Republic, depravation for the emperors,

catacombs for the Christians; with courage to conquer the whole world, and ambition to make all the nations of the earth into tributaries and suburbs . . ."

Truly the city had held gifts for all; but for freedom of the mind, for the banishment of care, for the exaltation of the spirit of man and the perfecting of his understanding, little or nothing.

"The civilization wafted from the East has here been made manifest in every form; here it is revealed in all its elements. But as touching the problem how man can live in freedom, that aspect has been neglected and the solution of that mysterious unknown can only be effected in the New World."

And then turning to Robinson "with shining eyes and heaving breast, flaming cheeks and fevered animation," he cried:

"I swear before you, I swear before the God of my fathers; by my fathers themselves, by my honour and by my country, that my arm shall not rest nor my mind be at peace until I have broken the chains which bind me, by the will and power of Spain."

The details of the journey back are obscure. The travellers seem to have gone down to Naples, and passed through Rome on the way back again. They paused for some time in Florence, where Bolívar sat down seriously to learn Italian and read the Florentine statesmen and historians. His delight in the Tuscan authors did not extend to Machiavelli; and O'Leary, his Irish aide-de-camp and biographer, who like many men of his time was an admirer of Italian literature, was shocked to find many years afterwards that the Liberator held "the common objection which has brought calumny on the name of that great Italian patriot and made it a symbol of every kind of political chicanery." Bolívar read *The Prince,* at any rate, and would willingly discuss it to the day of his death; but he never opened Machiavelli after leaving Florence. In London he read some Walter Scott, with no great pleasure, and amused himself in the grand manner, afterwards declaring that he had managed to spend 100,000 francs in three months. He was never very partial to London, but came to like it better when he returned there on a diplomatic mission in 1810—one of the three representatives of the first, short-lived, independent Republic of Venezuela.

Paris, which he had imagined to be the fountain of liberty, had been in the end a political disillusion. It was not in Paris that he beheld the vision of a liberated Spanish America, but in Rome, a city which had known nothing like liberty for eighteen centuries. There some dream of the future visited him; and later in his own country, when French ideals were receding before the difficulties of South American conditions, his thought tended more and more to classical Rome rather than revolutionary France. Neither was a "practical" or "realistic" view: both belonged to a mental, ideal world; Paris and Rome were countries of the mind. But experience drove him more and more to emphasize the Roman rather than the modern French element in his own ideal State, of which the romantic constitutions drafted in South America—for Angostura, for Colombia and for Bolivia—were only so many Platonic shadows. Was he a protesting dreamer with Shelley, a romantic man of action with Byron, playing at politics with unreal shapes and colours idly spread? No mere hard-headed practical realist could ever have done what Bolívar did.

Chapter Three

The First Venezuelan Republic

BOLÍVAR returned to Caracas in February 1807. The contrast between his ideals, acquired in Europe and from European books, with the actual conditions in South America which he found on his return, came with something of a shock. Humboldt's glib and superficial view of the readiness of the South American peoples for political liberty—so different from the careful observation and profundity of thought which he devoted to natural phenomena—proved to have no foundation in fact. Bolívar knew that the dominant part in the movement for emancipation was played by pure ideas, and that liberation (if it were ever to be achieved) would have to be the work of the educated Creoles. This is a fundamental fact in Bolívar's conception of how liberation could be achieved, and it was perhaps one of the causes of his ultimate failure. He himself was able enough and practical enough to recognize the contrast, and therefore to feel his failure all the more sharply. His mental background was romantic; he was to be the typical example—perhaps the greatest example—of the romantic man of action. But the romantic man of action is not blind to realities. He knows that the obstacles are there, but is confident that they can be overcome and overcome by himself. The essential thing is that he can make others believe it too: that they shall follow him everywhere and never leave him in the lurch. With loyalty, all things are possible—not necessarily the loyalty of all, but the loyalty of the chosen few. Bolívar was to fail in the end, not because he was incapable of inspiring loyalty—far from it—but because the loyalty he inspired was sometimes short-lived and the chosen few too few to rouse the indifferent and raise the self-seekers to the vision of something greater than their own welfare. Loyalty is a plant which lives on itself; it is used up in war, and seldom survives in peace.

Bolívar returned to Caracas to find that a filibustering expedition in the name of a free Venezuela had just been repulsed by the Spanish authorities. It was led by General Miranda.

Miranda was an adventurer, though an adventurer of genius, who with a number of other Spanish Americans had been at work in England, France and the United States, trying to interest the governments of those countries in the idea of revolution in the Spanish-American colonies. Miranda—"the great precursor," he has been called—was the most active of these revolutionaries. His plans had been taken seriously enough by the British Government for a pension to be granted him from Secret Service funds; and since the

Secret Service also paid the salary of his secretary, it was not unnatural that Miranda's letters should be intercepted and sometimes never reached their destination.

Miranda, born at Caracas in 1756, had joined the army in Spain, served in the war of American independence, and then held a command in the French revolutionary army under Dumouriez, the general who went over to the enemy. Miranda was court-martialled; but he was honourably acquitted, and his name is one of those inscribed on the Arc de Triomphe. In 1790 he was in touch with Pitt, and presented him with a plan for the future of Spanish-speaking America. This plan, wild and impracticable as it sounds, may be compared with Bolívar's far-sighted and more sensible schemes; the difference in intellectual outlook between the military adventurer in Miranda and the political thinker in Bolívar is strikingly apparent.

Miranda proposed a vast state whose northern boundaries would reach from the mouth of the Mississippi, to its headwaters on the 45th parallel, and then across to the Pacific. The southern boundary was to be Cape Horn, but Brazil and Guiana were carefully excluded. Government, modelled to a certain extent on Britain, was to be exercised by an hereditary emperor, an Inca. There was to be a House of Lords (or rather, of *Caciques*) [1] nominated by the Inca; while the

[1] Originally the word *Cacique* signified a chief in the West Indies.

House of Commons would be elected every five years. Judges would be life-appointments made by the Inca; and two Censors would be elected to watch over the behaviour of the Caciques in the Upper House and over the education of youth in the Empire. In addition to Censors, the new Inca Empire was to be provided with Ædiles and Quæstors on the Roman model; but in other respects, constitutional practice was to resemble that of Great Britain.

We may wonder why British statesmen lent so fantastic a scheme a measure of support. The reasons are not difficult to fathom. It was soundly monarchist, untainted by the republicanism of France or the United States; and it was unlikely to interfere with British interests, for no provision had been made for extending the new Inca Empire to Brazil, Guiana or any of the West Indian islands (except Cuba), which were possible spheres of British influence. We should remember that the extent of the British Empire had been greatly reduced by the loss of the North American colonies, and statesmen were on the look-out for some compensating addition in other parts of the world.

It was 15 years before General Miranda could even begin to undertake his plan of liberation. He had made his way to New York, where he collected a small expeditionary force; and in May 1806, about a month before Sir Home Popham's unfortunate descent on Buenos Aires, he reached the coast of Venezuela at Ocumare, hoping to surprise the Spanish garrison. Unfortunately for Miranda, information of the expedition and its movements had reached the Captain-General at Caracas through the Spanish Minister in Washington. Miranda's small force was overwhelmed as soon as it attempted to land, and he had to retire with the loss of two schooners and 60 men.

The British raid on Buenos Aires may have been part of a general plan for the emancipation of the Spanish colonies. Popham at any rate thought that it was, and believed that the capture of Buenos Aires would bring on the revolution at Caracas promised by Miranda. Unaware of Miranda's failure, he even invited him to come down to the River Plate and see for himself. A few weeks later the British expedition was expelled from Buenos Aires; and this double triumph for Spanish arms, in defending the Empire from foreign aggression, was duly celebrated in Caracas by a great religious festival. Miranda was burnt in effigy, and a price put upon his head. It is true that the Jesuits supported him; but they had been expelled from Spanish America in 1767, and favoured the plans of Miranda in the hope of returning to Venezuela when it should have obtained its independence.

Miranda, meanwhile, had reached Barbados, and attracted the attention of that picturesque old sea-dog, Admiral Cochrane. The governor of Trinidad helped him to prepare another invasion force of 15 vessels, and 400 volunteers. In spite of bad weather, they succeeded in landing near Coro; but the inhabitants (who had revolted ten years before and had been severely punished) were so little inclined to risk another revolution that Miranda sailed away without achieving anything at all. This time he turned to Jamaica; but there, neither the naval nor the military authorities were prepared to help him, and Miranda, in disgust, disbanded his force and returned to London.

Miranda had failed each time that he had led an expedition to Venezuela. There were several reasons for his failure. The most important, perhaps, was personal: he was not confident enough, or convincing enough, to inspire that unquestioning loyalty without which no commander can really succeed. He had been away for too long, and had lost touch with Venezuelan opinion; and though he had held an important command in the armies of revolutionary France, he had two fatal military defects: timidity in action and a tendency to give up before the first serious obstacle. He thought it would be enough for him to land on any beach in Spanish America, cry *Independencia!* and people would run to join him. Yet the fact of the matter was that a large number of Spanish Americans, including many of the half-white Pardos, were not interested in independence at all. They could see no good reason for political change. They would gain nothing in material prosperity, for they suffered little under Spanish rule, and were used to the procrastination and rigidity which were apt to retard colonial administration. They knew nothing of European ideas or political liberty, and thought that the only real enemy was the Creole landlord; and that meant that they took the part of the Spaniard against him and supported the Spanish Government.

Neither were the rich Creoles, themselves, particularly fond of Miranda, though it was they who were to bring in the revolution when it came four years later. Creole feeling against Miranda was not due to snobbery: to the fact that he was not one of the Creole aristocracy himself nor pretended to be; nor yet was it due to ignorance of his plans. In Caracas they knew a good deal more about Miranda's activity in London than was generally believed. They knew that he was financed by the British Government; and they feared that if the expedition succeeded, it would mean the practical domination of Venezuela by Britain and the loss of a good deal of their own importance.

That the Spanish colonists might one day demand autonomy had been foreseen as far back as 1783, by Aranda, the great minister of Charles III. He proposed to meet it (as will be seen later) by sending out Bourbon princes as viceroys who should in time become independent rulers—a scheme which had much in common with a similar plan for the British Empire, evolved by the elder Pitt; but it was rejected by Charles III, and Aranda fell from power.[1]

The revolutionary movement in Venezuela began in 1795 with a rising at Coro, a town some way from the capital and always in opposition to it. Serious outbreaks had already taken place in New Granada and Peru. On this occasion the causes of the revolt were social rather than political, although the influence of France and the United States is not difficult to detect. Negroes and Mulattos, with whom many Pardos and a few whites were secretly in touch, proclaimed what they called "the law of the French": a republican government, freedom for slaves, reduction of taxes. The rebels were overcome without difficulty and punished with the barbarous severity of the age.

Two years later (1797) a larger and more extensive conspiracy broke out under two Venezuelan Creoles: Gual and España. This time the aims were political as well as social, and likely to appeal to all classes except the Spaniards. The movement was definitely separatist. Gual and España claimed to restore to the South American people their lost liberty, with independence from Spain, remission of taxes, free trade, racial

[1] There is some evidence that Aranda's plan may have been a forgery.

equality, abolition of slavery, compulsory military training and the declaration of the Rights of Man. The ideology of this movement certainly came from abroad: the United States and France were examples to the Spanish colonies which seemed well worth following. But other influences were at work. Ideas of independence for Venezuela were spreading through contact with Englishmen interested in the economic development of the country as a market for English manufactured goods; and these wandering Englishmen—with the British fleet in the background—left no doubt in the minds of Venezuelans that a Creole was in every way the equal of a Spaniard from the Peninsula.

So if the ideas blowing in from revolutionary France helped to set the Spanish colonies on the course of revolt, their Creole leaders were encouraged by their own tradition, by North American example, by the British Navy in the Caribbean and by wandering Britons looking for markets. The "English intrigue" to which some historians have referred was largely the work of Miranda. He was the spirit moving official and public opinion in England, and aiming at British help for revolting Spanish colonies. The domination of Spain in America was illegal, he declared: an act of usurpation. The only legal title which the Spaniards could produce was a papal bull: "more a subject for jest than a matter for serious discussion."

Much of the modern interest in Miranda is due to the discovery, some twenty years ago, of his papers and correspondence which had come to rest in the library of an English country house. There was nothing discreditable in his taking English money. He devoted his life to the fight for freedom, and had to obtain support where he could find it. It has been supposed that he cherished a secret longing to be crowned Inca himself. He had commanded troops in the French Revolution, as Napoleon had. Napoleon had become an Emperor; why should not he, Miranda, become an Emperor too? His great mistake, which wrecked the whole plan, lay in not making sure of the support of the Creoles, the most influential class in the Colony—people who were reluctant to cut themselves adrift from the mother country, if it meant merely being taken in tow by another European power. The idea of emancipation from Spain was certainly there; but the Creoles were waiting for an opportunity, which they hoped might come in the confused situation of the Napoleonic wars.

The opportunity came with the events which took place in Spain in 1808. French troops entered the country on the pretext of passing through to Portugal; but they suddenly made for Madrid, while Napoleon demanded the cession of all the Spanish provinces north of the Ebro. In compensation Spain was to be given Portugal; while the Spanish royal family would go to

Mexico, in the way that the Portuguese Braganzas went to Rio de Janeiro—under the protection of the British Navy. The Bourbons were not equal to the emergency. Charles IV abdicated, and fled over the French frontier to Bayonne. Ferdinand VII, proclaimed King, lost his nerve and followed his father to France, where, on Napoleon's demand, he renounced all his newly won rights in favour of his father, who in turn made them over to Napoleon. This led to the accession of Joseph Bonaparte, Napoleon's brother, "the Intruder," who became King of Spain and of all the Spanish possessions in America.

The Spanish people had been kept entirely in the dark during these negotiations—treated as if they had no existence. Then they were told that the change was merely a change of dynasty; Spain would preserve the integrity of her dominions as well as her national independence. That was not good enough. On 2nd May, 1808 —*el dos de mayo*, a day that will always be remembered in Spain—the inhabitants of Madrid, with that reckless courage which distinguished them again in the Civil War of 1936–39, rose against the French army of occupation. They claimed, in the absence of their lawful King, that the sovereignty had reverted to the Spanish people, represented by the provincial and municipal councils; and these councils, or *juntas*, acting independently, proceeded to declare war on France and seek alliance with England.

News of these events caused consternation in Spanish America. At the beginning of July 1808 a post reached Caracas with several numbers of *The Times* and a report of the events in Bayonne. Andrés Bello was summoned to act as translator, but several members of the City Council believed the news to be false, until a high official in the Treasury told them firmly that neither the British Government nor *The Times* newspaper were capable of such deception. On 15th July a French corvette, the *Serpent*, reached La Guaira with two commissioners from King Joseph Bonaparte. They brought dispatches announcing the abdication of the Bourbon kings of Spain, and a note from the Council of the Indies ordering the colonists of Venezuela to recognize the new dynasty of Bonaparte. A few hours afterwards, a British frigate, the *Acasta*, also reached La Guaira; and while the French commissioners, in full-dress uniform, were explaining to the Spanish authorities at Caracas that they had now to accept Joseph I as King, Captain Beaver of the *Acasta* was dining at an inn, telling "all the respectable inhabitants of the city," (he said afterwards), what the real state of affairs in Spain was: how, in most Spanish provinces, *juntas* had been formed, and how a resistance movement had come into being against the French. His audience included what a Venezuelan writer of Spanish sympathies called "a crowd of seditious young men, youths whose ideas were opposed to monarchy: Sojos, Bolívares, Ribas . . ."—young Simón Bolívar, in fact, and many of his relations and friends who hailed Captain Beaver as their deliverer. The Spanish authorities escorted the Bonapartist commissioners down to La Guaira after dark; but Captain Beaver's second in command had the satisfaction of capturing the *Serpent* next morning.

Beaver reported to Admiral Cochrane that the Creoles were extremely loyal and passionately devoted to the Spanish branch of the House of Bourbon. So long as there was any probability of the return of Ferdinand to Madrid, they would remain united to the mother country; but if that did not take place within a reasonable time, he felt sure that they would declare themselves independent.

Captain Beaver was not far out. Opinion in Caracas was divided on what ought to be done. The City Council was in favour of a separate *junta* for the province of Venezuela, to act independently in the name of Ferdinand VII—"His Captive Majesty" they called him—in the same way that the provincial *juntas* were acting independently in Spain. The Spanish authorities in the colony preferred to recognize the *junta* of Seville—the most influential of the new Spanish regional councils—and to act on any instructions which the *junta* of Seville might send them. That solution did not content the Venezuelans, however. To begin with (as some of the Creoles immediately pointed out) it was bad law. According to the Laws of the Indies (the Statutes under which they all lived) the Spanish dominions overseas were joined to the Crown of Castille in a personal union; they had never been dependent on the Spanish Government. Charles IV had abdicated in favour of Ferdinand VII; so much was clear. But Ferdinand too had been deposed to make way for Joseph Bonaparte, and that would destroy the link which bound the colonies to the Crown, and so to the mother country. Secondly, they remarked on the inconvenience that would be caused by dependence on a council so far away as Seville. If the *junta* of Seville could act in the King's name as a kind of regency, so could theirs, and they clamoured for a *junta* of their own at Caracas. They would have protested their loyalty to Ferdinand VII as against Joseph Bonaparte; but since the link with the Crown had been broken by Ferdinand's deposition, the fact of independence from Spain implied a republic, and a republic was the form of government adopted by the two states by which their political thought was inspired: France and the United States.

Meanwhile the more alert spirits in Caracas were actively working against the Spanish Government. They were not in favour of following either the Captain-General or the City Council: neither had the authority to recognize the *junta* of Seville, they declared, and the idea of a conservative *junta* to maintain the rights of Ferdinand VII was abhorrent to them.

A patriotic debating society, the *Sociedad Patriótica*, held meetings of protest at a house in the country belonging to Bolívar. Only personal friends and members of the society were admitted; and, even then, one of them informed the police. The *Sociedad Patriótica* was suspected of holding extremist views: of being, in fact, a Jacobin Club, like those of the French Revolution. The sittings were held at another house, disguised as card-parties; and when these also were reported, the group came into the open and published a manifesto in favour of a separate *junta* for Caracas, independent of the one at Seville. The members knew very well that this was the first step towards independence from Spain, and Spaniards and their Venezuelan sympathizers found this attitude inconceivable. "It must be the first time," one of them wrote, "that a revolution can have been planned and carried out by those who had everything to lose by it. . . . These were no professional agitators, men of revolutions, who hoped to make money out of a state of disorder." The first leaders of South American emancipation from Spain belonged to the type represented by Shelley, Byron, and—allowing for the difference of mediæval surroundings—St. Francis of Assisi; the type sometimes known in England as the "Etonian Bolshevik."

In 1810 a new Captain-General arrived in

Caracas: Don Vicente Emparán. He was a capable and humane colonial official, who had been picked out for promotion by Napoleon himself, though in the end his appointment was made by the anti-Napoleonic *junta* at Seville. He was told that Bolívar was one of those who were trying to form an independent government for Venezuela, a *junta* analogous to those already formed in Spain. Emparán was a friend of Bolívar's family, and he privately told young Simón that it would be better for him to leave Caracas for a time. Bolívar had certainly been indiscreet: at a banquet at which the Captain-General was present he had raised his glass to the toast of South American independence. He did, however, leave Caracas, and that prevented him from taking any active part in the movement against Emparán.

In general the Spanish authorities in America inclined to recognize Joseph Bonaparte; Venezuela and Mexico were exceptional in that they did not do so. But the great majority of the Spanish American people made noisy demonstrations of loyalty to the Spanish Bourbon dynasty; and at the beginning of the French invasion Spanish Americans sent to Spain as much as 70,000 pesos (dollars) to help the resistance movement against Napoleon. But events moved faster than anyone expected. The occupation of Southern Spain and Andalucía by Joseph Bonaparte, in January 1810, brought down the *Junta Suprema* which had been sitting at Seville; it was replaced by a Council of Regency which met at Cadiz and summoned the Cortes: the Spanish parliament. A stirring proclamation by the Spanish poet Quintana had effects which were unexpected. It had been meant to unite the Empire in one; but, by accepting as truths the hostile reports on the Spanish colonial system, it opened the doors to separatism and provided some justification for the revolutionary argument. "From this moment, Spanish Americans, you see yourselves free men. . . . Your destinies no longer depend on ministers, viceroys or governors; they are in your own hands." The Spanish Americans took him at his word.

On the morning of 19th April, 1810, which was Holy Thursday (the Thursday next before Easter), members of the City Council of Caracas, who had assembled for church, took the new Captain-General by surprise by demanding an extraordinary meeting. A proposal was made for forming a *junta* and for inviting him to preside. They were on the point of voting, and some were already applauding the new chairman, when they were interrupted by Dr. Cortés de Madariaga, a Chilean and a canon of the cathedral, but not a member of the Council. Claiming to speak for the clergy, he delivered an impassioned appeal in favour of an autonomous Venezuelan government. The Captain-General rose, and went out on to the balcony. He was personally not unpopular, and there were people in the crowd in the square outside who were willing to support him. But when he asked the question: "Do you wish me to remain with you as Governor?" the canon stood behind him, making signs and grimaces that they should say "No." Emparán shrugged his shoulders and accepted the situation; there was not much else that he could do. He was escorted down to La Guaira and put on board a Spanish man-of-war. The first independent government in South America had come into being. Buenos Aires followed on 25th May, 1810, Santa Fe de Bogotá on 20th July, Santiago de Chile on 18th September, and by the end of 1810 all the capitals of Spanish-speaking America had done the same, with the sole exception of Lima (Peru) and Guatemala. It should be noted that the province of Venezuela had started on its career of self-government in the name of Ferdinand VII, without recognizing the authority of the Council of Regency at Cadiz. That implied the assumption of political power in Venezuela by the municipalities: the City Council of Caracas and the town and provincial councils elsewhere.

One of the first cares of the new government was to send properly accredited diplomatic agents to London. The mission was entrusted to Colonel Simón Bolívar, assisted by Luis López Méndez, whom Bolívar afterwards described, in an outburst of characteristic generosity, as "the real liberator of America." The Secretary of Legation was Andrés Bello, once Bolívar's tutor, who stayed in London for twenty years and became the cultural focus as well as the political centre of all the Spanish Americans in the metropolis.

The mission could not be received officially by the British Foreign Secretary, Lord Wellesley; Britain was at peace with Spain and in alliance with her. So the South Americans were received privately at Apsley House. Their credentials and the instructions they had received from their government had been drafted with studied moderation, in view of the theoretical legal rights of the King of Spain who was a prisoner in France. Venezuela, a part of the Spanish Empire, desired the protection of the British Navy against attack from the French; in return they were prepared to offer Britain substantial commercial advantages. The friendliness with which the mission had been received encouraged Bolívar to mention another matter: independence. It has been claimed that he acted with undue precipitation, and was guilty of an indiscretion in raising the question of independence without authority to do so. Actually he referred to the matter in the form which his instructions prescribed and followed them closely, as is shown by the copy of the instructions which has been preserved. Wellesley urged the mission to adopt a policy of conciliation towards Spain; but Bolívar and López Méndez argued that the provisional government of Venezuela was the only one which could preserve the rights of Ferdinand VII against usurpation by the French. A few days later (21st July, 1810) Bolívar and López Méndez provided Lord Wellesley with a written statement of the object of their mission; and on 8th August Wellesley forwarded an account of the conversation which had taken place to Bolívar, sending at the same time (as diplomatic etiquette demanded) a copy to the Spanish Embassy.

All that could be done at the moment for "the ambassadors of South America," as *The Times* and *The Morning Chronicle* called them, was to instruct British commanders on the West Indian Station to take any measures they might think fit to support the governments in America, whatever they might be, against the intrigues, peaceful penetration or open aggression of the French. British policy had two main objects: the prosecution of the war against Napoleon, and the development of commerce. It was only after Napoleon had been defeated that the British Government could support the Spanish colonies in their rebellion against Spain, for reasons which were purely economic.

Meanwhile the Venezuelan mission had a considerable social success, as its visitors' book showed. They dined with the Duke of Gloucester; they drove down Bond Street and in the Park in a splendid equipage; they were seen at the Opera and at Astley's Circus. Bolívar was painted by at least one fashionable portrait-painter. Miranda took him to see Wilberforce, liberator of the slaves. They visited the Royal Observatory, and a training-college for teachers established by the great educational reformer Joseph Lancaster; they resolved to send two young Venezuelan teachers to England to be educated in the principles and practice of the Lancastrian system.

The Spanish Embassy heard of their doings with considerable annoyance. The Regency Council in Cadiz declared the Venezuelans rebels, and ordered all the ports of "those treacherous provinces" to be blockaded. This decision was due mainly to the influence of the Cadiz merchants, who did not like the idea of ports in Spanish America being open to trade with other countries than Spain, and least of all with Great Britain. Bolívar wrote an article for *The Morning Chronicle*, explaining the circumstances and protesting against the blockade. There was considerable resentment among exporters in England, too; and the blockade was one of the facts which weighed most heavily with Castlereagh when, later, came the question of recognition.

Bolívar sailed for Venezuela in September 1810 in a British man-of-war, followed—in the ordinary packet—by Miranda. The object of their travelling separately was probably to avoid calling attention to their relationship. There was the further consideration, however, that Lord Wellesley did not like the idea of Miranda sailing in the same ship as Bolívar: he asked him to put off his departure for eight or ten days, while the Spanish Ambassador tried to extract a pledge from Wellesley that Miranda should not be allowed to sail at all. Many people in Venezuela, also, distrusted Miranda; they had not forgotten his failure at Coro in 1806, and the members of Bolívar's diplomatic mission had been warned against him. Bolívar, however, did not hesitate to enter into conversation with Miranda or even to invite him to return to Venezuela; he believed that Miranda was "the man the revolution wanted." It might have been better if he had heeded the warning. But at first all went well. Miranda returned to Venezuela; Bolívar gave him hospitality in his own house at Caracas, and did what he could to extend his influence. The *generalísimo*, as they called him, was imposing in appearance and irresistible in argument, but he was unable to act resolutely in a crisis. Reports of his military qualities may have been exaggerated, and age had weakened his constitution. Bolívar respected him as the first man who had seriously tried to deliver Venezuela from oppression; but not many of his countrymen shared Bolívar's enthusiasm, or were impressed by Miranda's reputation in Europe. Both Miranda and Bolívar were coldly received by the *Junta*; but Miranda was presently made Lieutenant-

General, and elected a member of the new Congress of Venezuela.

On 5th July, 1811, Congress published the declaration of Venezuelan Independence; the representatives of the "United Provinces forming the American confederation of Venezuela" . . . "in full and absolute possession of our rights which we recovered justly and legitimately after 19th April, 1810, in consequence of the events of Bayonne and the occupation of the Spanish throne by conquest, and the succession of a new dynasty constituted without our consent," had determined to make use of the rights "of which we have been deprived by force for more than three centuries."

The Constitution was adopted the following December. It pleased the politically minded minority; but the mass of the people did not understand the change or see why it had been made; it seemed much the same to them whether the ruling oligarchy was Creole or Spanish. Congress, instead of trying to grasp the main problems, became entangled in theoretical discussion and constitutional conundrums, although the mandate received by many deputies from their constituencies was, before everything else, to make certain of the Republic's safety and independence. And, as a matter of fact, counter-revolution was being prepared under their very noses; at Coro and Valencia it broke out a few days after the Declaration of Independence, and a force (in which Bolívar was a volunteer) moving against the rebels was repelled and had to return without anything being accomplished.

Caracas now turned to Miranda, the only man to help them in the emergency. But Miranda was in no hurry to oblige them. "Where are the forces," he asked, "which a general of my seniority can command without compromising his reputation?"

Eventually he accepted the command, but would not allow Bolívar to be included in the expedition; although Bolívar went, after all, as aide-de-camp to the Marqués del Toro, and Miranda won a small success by capturing Valencia. Yet every day he became more difficult. He would not accept local conditions, nor try to understand the character and temper of the men he had to command. Brought up on older, pre-Napoleonic principles of warfare, he refused to consider anything new, or anything suggested by officers who were junior to him; and Miranda was not only very much senior in rank, but also very much older in years than any of the other officers with whom he had to serve. Bolívar, and some of the younger Venezuelan officers, had a far clearer sense of what could be done with the Venezuelan soldier, who was not distinguished for discipline or at "doing things by numbers," but made an excellent guerrilla-fighter or scout. They knew, as well as Miranda, the value of mechanical discipline. It was that kind of disciplined routine, carried out under fire—and with considerable loss—which enabled the British Legion to save the situation long afterwards at Carabobo; and there are stories of disciplined Spanish regulars in Venezuela, resisting back to back—*culo a culo*, the phrase was—until they fell where they stood. Miranda knew the value of such discipline, but he did not realize that it cannot be improvised. Bolívar, on the contrary, and other Venezuelan commanders, tried to get the best out of the Venezuelan soldier in a short time by exploiting his good qualities; instead of training raw recruits in the Prussian style, like Miranda, they set to work to train them to be guerrillas.

The local commanders on the other side quickly learnt the same lesson. From the first, the cause of Spanish reaction attracted all kinds of irresponsible adventurers, who were guilty of frightful atrocities. The two most famous—or infamous—were Monteverde and Boves. Monteverde, a Spanish naval man, a petty officer, presented himself to the Captain-General with a plan for raiding the province of Caracas, in something the same way that the English had in the sixteenth century—the raid under Amyas Leigh (or Amyas Preston) so vividly described by Charles Kingsley in *Westward Ho!* Monteverde did even better, for, like some of the Spanish conquistadores, he was joined by a friendly Indian who had been given command of a Venezuelan outpost and then went over to the Spaniards. The Spanish Royalists had never lost the Venezuelan part of Guiana on the East, nor Coro nor Maracaibo on the North-West; and Monteverde was about to make his raid on the centre, when the forces of reaction received an overwhelming support from the forces of nature.

On Holy Thursday, 26th March, 1812, two years after that other Holy Thursday when the Captain-General had given way to the first Venezuelan *Junta*, Caracas and many other towns held by the Venezuelan Republicans were destroyed by one of the worst earthquakes in history. The shocks came at a time in the afternoon when many people were in church and the troops confined to barracks; the loss of life was very heavy.

To Monteverde, it seemed a heaven-sent opportunity for destroying the enemy, and he pushed on vigorously with his raid. In one town, though the barracks were full of dead and wounded, the arms and ammunition were untouched. Monteverde appropriated these, as well as the guns of a Republican battery. It was certainly very curious that the towns held by the Royalists had hardly suffered from the earthquake at all; and monks and priests lost no time in attributing the earthquake to the wrath of God against the red Republicans: "the scourge of an irritated Deity against the innovators who had rejected that most virtuous of monarchs,

Ferdinand VII, the Lord's annointed." They stood preaching to the frightened crowds among the ruins, addressing themselves particularly to those who were living in sin, and frightening them still more.

Bolívar's house, like many others, was in ruins; the first floor had fallen in and the doors had been torn off their hinges, leaving everything at the mercy of thieves and looters. He collected some friends, and as many of his household slaves as he could find—for, like everyone else who could afford it, he kept slaves too—and turned them into stretcher-bearers. He went from one end of the city to the other, comforting the wounded, and having the dead burnt or buried. He saw a monk climb on to a broken table, and begin to use it as a pulpit. He pulled him down, and threatened to kill him if he did not stop talking. "I saw Bolívar," a hostile witness said afterwards, "on a heap of ruins, climbing about in his shirt-sleeves. He saw me, and shouted these impious and extravagant words: 'If nature is against us, we will fight against that too, and make it do what we want.' " Impious or extravagant, those words might have been the motto for Bolívar's whole career. He was as shocked and stirred by the earthquake at Caracas as Voltaire had been by the earthquake at Lisbon.

The Republican government of Venezuela fell back on a military dictatorship. An economic dictatorship would have been more to the point.

Neither the patriotism of the *Generalísimo* nor his military or administrative qualities were enough to check the economic confusion, the political reaction and the enemy at the gate. Miranda was hardly the man to overcome the obstacles which a dictator had to face, and beat the enemy in Venezuela at the same time. He had lived too long abroad; his thought and his language seemed to belong to a different world; he had lost touch with the customs of his own country, and was completely at sea in social surroundings so different from any of those to which he had been accustomed in the capitals of Europe. Yet the disaster, when it came, was not due entirely to timidity and lack of determination. He had to reckon with the obstruction of civil servants in the province of Caracas, and the lack of loyalty of some of the commanders in the field. Above all, people at large were still indifferent to independence, or even opposed to it.

Under the dictatorship of Miranda things went from bad to worse. Some Republican commanders went over to the Royalists; some of Bolívar's friends (including his wife's relations) declined to serve under Miranda's orders. Bolívar, now colonel, was packed off to command the dingy stronghold of Puerto Cabello. In the castle outside the town were a number of Royalist prisoners: and one day, when the commandant of the castle happened to be absent, a Venezuelan lieutenant went over to the Royalists, freed the prisoners, hoisted the Royal Standard, and turned his guns on Bolívar at the port. Bolívar held out for a week, against the castle and a detachment of Royalist troops which had arrived from Valencia. He reported to Miranda that a combined operation might be possible to take the besieging forces in front and rear; but his message reached Miranda too late, and six days afterwards Bolívar, with only 40 men left, embarked them for La Guaira, and Puerto Cabello fell.

The loss of Puerto Cabello was a great discouragement to the Republican command. Miranda still had more men under arms than Monteverde—one of his first acts on becoming commander-in-chief had been to order universal conscription; but his levies were ill-trained and his officers inspired him with little confidence. The situation was by no means desperate, but he lost heart. To the surprise and consternation of the whole of Venezuela, he suddenly capitulated, without consulting any of his officers or any member of the government. He proposed a negotiated peace, guaranteeing the lives and property of all Venezuelans. The Declaration of Independence had been premature, he decided.

The capitulation was signed on 25th July, 1812; it included an amnesty for political offences and the provision of passports for any who wished to leave the country. "By these articles," says Professor W. S. Robertson, the biographer of

Miranda, "the generalissimo of a revolutionary army of some 4,500 men capitulated to an upstart loyalist who commanded forces that were evidently inferior in numbers." Contemporary evidence was generally hostile to Miranda; it is only lately that attempts have been made to justify him—at Bolívar's expense. Alexander Scott, who had been entrusted by the United States with food for those who had suffered from the earthquake, reported to Secretary Monroe (who had not yet become president) that Miranda, "by a shameful and treacherous capitulation" surrendered the liberties of his country. "Whether [he adds] he was an agent of the British Government, as he now states, or whether this conduct resulted from a base and cowardly heart, I cannot decide." The charge that he betrayed his country depends on his relations with the Marqués de Casa León, a Venezuelan who went over to the Spaniards, and was rewarded for his conduct by the Spanish commander.

The most charitable explanation of Miranda's action is that he was taking gold with him, the property of the Venezuelan Republic, for deposit in a place of safety. He had avoided discussing the subject with Monteverde; and (in the words of George Robertson, the English merchant to whom the gold was delivered) "the floating property of the State of Venezuela was not at all stipulated to be given up, but that he intended that it should afford a conveyance for the unfortunate inhabitants to some friendly or allied port." Miranda, it is stated, was looking towards New Granada, where he counted Nariño as his friend. He believed that he could invade Venezuela from the west and regain Caracas—as Bolívar was to do, later; unfortunately he did not make his intention known to any of his colleagues and guerrilla warfare was as distasteful to him as it was to Napoleon.

Miranda did not wait to surrender to Monteverde in person, or see that the terms of the capitulation were carried out. It would hardly be fair to say that he doubted Monteverde's good faith; but he decided to leave Venezuela himself before the Royalist leader occupied Caracas. He abandoned his troops, passed through Caracas a few hours ahead of Monteverde, and reached La Guaira where a British ship, H.M.S. *Sapphire*, was waiting to take him off. The captain wished him to come aboard at once, so that he could sail at dawn with the off-shore breeze. But Miranda was tired, and decided to sleep on shore. The decision was fatal; it cost him his liberty and his life.

The capitulation had been received with dismay by many Republicans, especially by the officers. They thought it unnecessary. It may be true, as General Miller remarks in his *Memoirs*, that some of the richer and more influential inhabitants of the country were withholding their support; not that their political sentiments had undergone a change, but because they saw the uselessness of sacrificing life and property "in a wild attempt to stem the stream of public opinion." The bulk of the people, he adds, had become decidedly royalist in principle ever since the earthquake, "which had been represented by the priesthood as a judgment of heaven upon the insurgent cause."

O'Leary, Bolívar's Irish A.D.C., gives in his *Memoirs* the view of officers serving at the time, though he did not himself reach the country until long after. Discipline, and their respect for Miranda, had prevented them hitherto from giving open expression to their opinions; the capitulation left them free to say what they liked. Among the most indignant was Bolívar himself. For Miranda, the Commander-in-Chief, to leave Caracas without waiting for Monteverde, he regarded as treachery; for he foresaw only too clearly the dangers to which such a step would expose any Venezuelan who had fought in the Republican army. Miranda's desertion invited, and even authorized, a violation of the terms which Monteverde had accepted.

Bolívar tried at first to use his personal influence, his powers of persuasiveness, to prevent commanding officers from demobilizing their troops. He was unsuccessful, and went down to La Guaira, with three other officers, two colonels and a major, determined to prevent Miranda from getting away. At the port, they heard a rumour that the ship had taken on board a large sum of money; and they jumped to the conclusion—which seems to have been unjustified, in the light of further knowledge—that that, too, was connected with Miranda's evasion. They arrested Miranda in bed, and handed him over to the Commandant of the port, who surrendered him to Monteverde the next day. He was sent to Spain, in irons, and died miserably in a dungeon at Cadiz.

No action of Bolívar's life has been more criticized than this; but the critics, living and writing in times of peace, in a world far from the ruthless logic of war and the passionate unreason of defeat, have not been in a position to understand what it felt like—to Bolívar and others—for the Commander-in-Chief to sign a capitulation over their heads and then try to get away. The circumstances were in some ways not unlike those of Dunkirk in 1940—or, for that matter, Bruges and Ostend in 1914—where any commander who had done what Miranda did would certainly have been shot.

Some of Bolívar's English contemporaries felt in the same way. Although to General Miller Bolívar seemed to have been "hurried into dreadful error by the warmth of his feelings," to Colonel Belford Wilson Bolívar always asserted that it "was solely his own act, to punish the *treachery and treason* of Miranda in capitulating to an inferior force, and then intending to embark, himself knowing that the capitulation would not be observed." Earlier, Colonel Wilson had written that Leandro (the general's son) "has promised to let me peruse some justificatory documents concerning his father, and I shall ask for copies. General Bolívar always *gloried* to me in having risked his own safety which he might have secured by embarking on board a vessel, in order to secure the punishment of Miranda for his alleged treason. His plea was not altogether ill-founded, for he argued that if Miranda believed the Spaniards would observe the treaty, he should have remained to keep them to their word; if he did not, he was a traitor to have sacrificed his army to it. General Bolívar invariably added that he wished to shoot Miranda as a traitor, but was withheld by the others."

At dawn orders came that no ship was to leave the port. The *Sapphire* was already under way, and the Republicans were caught; the Commandant had gone over to the Royalists.

Many Venezuelan officers were imprisoned by Monteverde, or shot. Others managed to get away and to rejoin the Republicans later; and that was what happened to Bolívar. Through influential friends at Caracas, he was granted a passport to leave the country; but it was nearly refused when he declared that the arrest of Miranda was intended to punish a traitor, not to serve the King of Spain. Monteverde did not think Bolívar important enough to prevent him going;

but there was nothing approaching an amnesty, and the capitulation was treated like the proverbial scrap of paper.

Bolívar with his passport reached Curaçao, then under British occupation. A few other Republicans, some with passports and some without, managed to escape to various islands in the West Indies. By the end of 1812, Venezuela had returned to the condition of a Spanish colony, worse off, under the insensate tyranny of Monteverde, than it had ever been before.

O'Leary relates in his *Memoirs* that Bolívar thought at the time of going to England and offering to serve under Sir Arthur Wellesley, soon to be the Duke of Wellington. Whether he really meant it, or whether it was an idea that passed through his mind, or whether he said so to disguise his real intentions, the plan was prevented by the sequestration of his property by Monteverde, and by the loss of his luggage (and all his ready money) in the British Customs. What little baggage he had was detained through having been deposited in the same shed as that of Miranda; and his money was withheld to meet debts contracted when he was commanding at Puerto Cabello.

Bolívar set out on his career of liberation practically penniless.

Chapter Four

The Reconquest of Venezuela

BOLÍVAR had learnt that his mission in life was to liberate his country from Spain; and that meant making himself a soldier, a commander of regular and irregular troops, and at the same time a diplomat, a statesman and an international political thinker. But it also meant the hardest task of all: to be strong in adversity and never despair in defeat.

On this occasion he had been defeated not only by the Spaniards but by the physical and mental conditions of the Venezuelans themselves. Sarmiento, the elementary schoolmaster who became President of the Argentine Republic, put it well when he said that in South America two civilizations existed side by side. One, which was coming to birth, had no knowledge of what it had against it and was like the simple-minded popular civilization of the early middle ages. The other, without noticing what was happening at its very doors, was trying to do in South America what was being done at the same time in Europe. It was as if the twelfth century and the nineteenth existed side by side, one in the towns and the other in the country.

This condition is clearly shown in the wars of independence. There was first of all the war of the towns against the Spaniards, begun by Creoles full of European ideas in order to give their ideas scope for development; and then there was the war of the *caudillos* (the rough irregular leaders) against the towns, in order to free themselves from all civil control, give free rein to their own lawless character and way of life, and show that European civilization was a thing which they heartily despised. First, the towns won against the Spaniards, and then the country won against the towns. But, in Venezuela, there was a further complication; for there, the *caudillos* raised the countryside against the towns to fight for Spain, and that was the side of the war which brought most destruction and loss of life. In the end, both the country and the towns joined Bolívar to drive the Spaniards out; but the beginnings were hard, and the penniless liberator got little sympathy and no support.

Curaçao was unfriendly to Bolívar, at Government House as well as in the Customs. He eventually made his way to Cartagena, the old fortified seaport on the Gulf Coast of New Granada, and offered his services to that Republic, which also had thrown off the Spanish dominion. Meanwhile he sat down to write a *Memoria* to the citizens, an explanation of the failure of the Republicans in Venezuela, urging the inhabitants of the two countries to unite against the common enemy.

It is curious that two neighbouring Spanish dominions should have developed so strong a sense of regionalism that they felt foreigners to one another, before they had even made sure of their independence from Spain. Yet such a feeling of local nationalism was quite consistent with loyalty to the Spanish Crown; for the territories were not considered to be provinces, but kingdoms, and the full title of New Granada had been "The New *Kingdom* of Granada." The different parts of the Spanish Empire (as already stated in the first chapter) were not annexed to Spain, but incorporated in the Spanish Crown without losing any of their rights or privileges. The dominions were nominally independent of Spain in Europe; and it was upon this principle that South Americans, after Ferdinand's imprisonment by Napoleon, had claimed an equal right with Spain to elect *juntas* of their own, which should act in absence of "His captive Majesty," King Ferdinand VII, their only legal head. Then, by a natural process, the inborn sense of separatism acted again; and the *juntas*, considering that—with the continued absence of the King and the occupation of the throne by conquest—the sovereignty had reverted to the people, determined to make use of their rights and had proclaimed a republic.

Bolívar, then, when he sat down to write the

Memoria de Cartagena was addressing a new republic. The *Memoria* is a remarkable document. It already shows Bolívar's political genius: that blend of burning, intellectual idealism and practical diplomatic common sense which distinguish him from other liberators. The *Memoria* is a programme for the future, not a mere crying over spilt milk. In Bolívar's opinion, the fundamental mistake of the Venezuelan Republicans had lain in their complacency and inaction, their tendency to take things as they were. To begin with: the *Junta*, instead of capturing and occupying the Royalist stronghold of Coro—which it could easily have accomplished from the sea, eight miles off—had allowed the place to be fortified, so that in the end it became the base from which the whole Republic was subjugated. The *Junta* had founded its policy on humanitarian principles; but it did not understand their implications: it could not force freedom on a people unaware of their rights. Rather than cope with the practical problems of administration and government, they had been dreaming of a republic in the clouds, and had tried to achieve political perfection by assuming the human race to be little short of perfect itself.

> "In this way we have had *philosophes* instead of leaders, philanthropy instead of legislation, dialectics instead of tactics, and sophists instead of soldiers."

Treasonable acts had gone unpunished, particularly on the part of the Spaniards who had been allowed to remain in the country and had kept it in a perpetual state of unrest, promoting endless conspiracies and always getting off with a free pardon. Every conspiracy was followed by a pardon, and every pardon by another conspiracy, pardoned again in its turn because it was said that liberal governments should be distinguished for their clemency. Criminal clemency, he called it; for it had done more than anything to wreck the machinery of government, almost before that machinery was in working order. Then, again, instead of raising and training a disciplined body of troops, while there was still time, they had hastily improvised innumerable bands of undisciplined militia; and these, besides wasting public money on the pay and allowances of the higher ranks, had ruined the country's agriculture by taking workers from the land, bringing odium on the government, because it had compelled these men to take up arms and leave their families. Bolívar's criticism of the military policy of the Republic is harsh, but true; he too was learning.

Republics, it was said, had no need to pay men for preserving their liberties; when the enemy attacked, every citizen would become a soldier. In Venezuela, the result had shown how far out that calculation was; for the militiamen who went out to meet the enemy often did not know how to handle their weapons, and, being unused to discipline or to obeying any kind of orders, they were crushed at the very beginning of the campaign, in spite of the heroic efforts made by some of their officers to lead them to victory.

So much for the military mistakes. Other mistakes of the same kind had been made in regard to administration. The dissipation of public funds in frivolous and prejudicial objects—and particularly in the salaries of an infinite number of clerks, secretaries, law-officers, provincial and federal officials—had dealt a mortal blow to the Republic because it obliged them to fall back upon "the perilous expedient of paper money," with no other backing than force and the imaginary revenues of the State. A million pesos had been issued by 1811, based on import duties and the tobacco monopoly; but as funds for redemption were lacking, the notes steadily depreciated in value. Bolívar's remarks on the psychological effects of paper money in Venezuela are very interesting. That new form of currency seemed in the eyes of most people a clear violation of the rights of property; for they saw themselves deprived of objects of intrinsic value in exchange for something whose value was uncertain and even illusory. The paper money was the crowning disillusion of the solid and respectable people of the interior; and they sometimes called in the commander of the nearest Spanish troops to come and deliver them from a kind of money which they regarded with far more horror than subjection to Spain.

As if this were not enough, there was the earthquake, which, Bolívar said, had exasperated the feelings of the fanatics and increased the influence of the clergy, "always ready to lend their support to any form of despotism."

Last of all, there was federalism. The Venezuelan Constitution of 1811 had been modelled on the United States Constitution of 1787 and the French declaration of the Rights of Man, while the political organization followed that of the United States in adopting the principle of state sovereignty. That, in the eyes of Bolívar, was one of the rocks on which they had been wrecked. It might well be the most perfect system from the point of view of human happiness, but it was opposed to all the interests of an infant republic like theirs.

> "It is essential that the government should be suited to the circumstances, the times, and the men. If these are calm and prosperous, the State should be gentle and protective; but if they are turbulent and calamitous, the government must show itself strong, and arm itself to meet those dangers, without waiting for laws and constitutions, until at any rate it has established peace and happiness."

It is clear from these statements that Bolívar was no doctrinaire, like Miranda. "The Precursor (it has been said) believed the Constitution to be the panacea for all public calamities; the Liberator always had a somewhat mitigated confidence in the virtue of legal precepts." For Bolívar, there was now one form of constitution, and one form only, which could be recommended to a civilized state.

Bolívar understood that the most important thing was to make sure of the liberties of individual citizens, and "not to expect miracles of Liberty with a capital L." He always called attention to the danger of the turbulent conditions produced by revolutionary idealism preached by demagogues. He knew only too well how ignorant some of the South American peoples were, how little understanding there was between the various races, and how royalist Spanish propaganda had aggravated racial jealousy. Knowing the lack of political experience of the people and the huge extent of the country, he stood for a strong government which might make some liberty possible to everyone. They could see what had happened to the First Venezuelan Republic, "with its craze for imitation," its "picturesque ideologies," and its "tardy *generalísimo*." Bolívar saw that the first thing was to create an army. The intellectual in him realized that he would have to become a soldier. "Military instruction and training are indispensable for us. The political doctrines which have so far prevailed are unsuited to our social conditions and our mental development. Our citizens have never had any training in the virtues which belong to the true republican."

The immediate need, of course, was to ensure the safety of New Granada, and that depended on the reconquest of Venezuela. They must become allies against the common enemy, and carry the war into the enemy's country. "Every defensive war," he said with truth, "is ruinous for those who have to maintain it: it weakens without hope of indemnification, while hostilities in enemy country can always be profitable, from the good which comes of evil inflicted on the enemy." Bolívar was now to prove the truth of this; for with a few hundred troops from New Granada he was to carry the war in three months from the Colombian border to Caracas.

After the capitulation and imprisonment of Miranda, the exile of Bolívar and the death or silence of most of the influential Republicans, the whole of Venezuela had fallen once more under Spanish domination. The Spanish Government in Europe (which had no idea of what sort of man its self-appointed representative was) instructed Monteverde to promulgate the Constitution of Cadiz; but though this was duly promulgated at Caracas at the end of 1812, Monteverde decided on his own authority to apply only what he called "the law of conquest." During his twelve months' dictatorship, there was no crime or outrage that was not committed. Monteverde and his associates—adventurers rather than regular soldiers—had Republicans shot right and left. "I assure you, sir, that not one of these Creoles shall escape, if I can get my hands on them. All this 'politics' must be stopped at once. We have nothing to do with a regency or a cortes or a constitution, but with our own security and the extermination of all these insurgents and bandits. I know that you can't finish with all of them; but you can finish with any who might become leaders; and for the rest, it's Puerto Rico, Havana, or Spain for them." Such was the letter or report, dictated from Rio Caribe, on 18th June, 1813, by Cerveriz, a typical example of the kind of man to whom Spain—unknown to the liberal-minded Cortes of Cadiz—owed the preservation of her empire at that time.

The Republicans replied by the proclamation of *guerra a muerte*, "war to the death." The Spaniards had never recognized the Venezuelans as belligerents; they had treated them as rebels, and had frequently exercised the right of putting to death any persons found with arms in their hands. The South Americans, on the contrary, had given quarter to the Royalists whom they captured. The effect of this was that many South Americans preferred to serve with the Royalists, feeling sure that if they were taken prisoner their lives would be spared. Bolívar realized the great disadvantage under which he laboured; and as a reprisal for the butcheries committed—not so much by the Spaniards, as by the irregular commanders and troops who defended their cause—he issued a proclamation (15th June, 1813) declaring that, from that time forward, he would give no quarter. This declaration of *guerra a muerte* on the part of the Republicans made the danger of all prisoners being shot equal on both sides. The *guerra a muerte* actually originated with one of the mildest of men: Antonio Nicolás Briceño, a learned lawyer and member of the first Venezuelan Congress, well known to Bolívar. Escaping to Cartagena, Briceño collected a group of volunteers, or partisans, to make reprisal raids into Venezuela, and kill every Spaniard and Canary Islander they came across. They went up to Cúcuta, just inside the border of New Granada, where they found Bolívar.

With his usual impulsive manner Bolívar had lost no time. Rapidity of decision and swiftness of action were two of his greatest military qualities. Having joined the army of New Granada in December 1812, he had already conducted successful not to say brilliant operations on the upper reaches of the River Magdalena. He had been promoted brigadier-general, and accorded the rights of citizenship, and was at that moment awaiting instructions from the government of New Granada to invade Venezuela. He accepted the *guerra a muerte*, though with important reservations. Spaniards would only be shot if found with arms actually in their hands; others should be made to march with the Republican forces, where they could be kept under observation. The proclamation was a reply to numerous acts of the most abominable cruelty, and would make sure that none who were South American-born could be indifferent to the struggle. Bolívar also wished to get rid of the idea that the war was one between plantation-owners and rebellious slaves, which was not the case; it was not a civil war but an international one. People should know that to be South American-born was one thing: to be a Spaniard or a Canary Islander, quite another. They were intruders; and a mistake might cost a man his life.

"Bolívar's mind," a Venezuelan writer has remarked, "was in some respects very Spanish; and it was never more Spanish than at this moment. His terrible steely eloquence, and his inflexible attitude in the presence of death, are not so much that of an individual of Spanish descent as that of the whole Spanish race." Bolívar's declaration of war to the death was Spanish in another way. There he was, with no more than a handful of patriots to follow him—at the time of the proclamation he had only 600—declaring war on the whole Spanish Empire, a gesture which makes him comparable with Cortés and the greatest of the Spanish conquistadores. "He was incapable of shedding a drop of blood for pleasure," a Peruvian once said of him, "but he would have shed the blood of the whole world if he thought it necessary for the independence of South America." His energy was not cruelty, and his inflexibility was never the pleasure in evil for its own sake. Even after the proclamation, he did not immediately put war to the death into practice.

Bolívar crossed the Venezuelan border as an independent commander, and invaded the provinces of Mérida and Trujillo (May 1813). His men had come mainly from New Granada; and they included two of the most gallant regimental officers of the whole war: Atanacio Girardot and Antonio Ricaurte. Briceño had already gone on; but he was attacked unexpectedly by one of the cut-throat Royalist leaders, taken prisoner, and shot. The Spanish governor of the province had already announced that he would give no quarter, and Bolívar could only threaten further reprisals. The Spanish—or at least their irregular leaders—had, Bolívar declared in a proclamation of 15th June, 1813, violated the law of nations, broken the terms of a capitulation and the most solemn treaties, committed every crime and reduced Venezuela to utter desolation. Justice, he said, demanded reprisals, and necessity obliged him to carry them out.

The *guerra a muerte* actually favoured the Royalists more than the Republicans, for the Spaniards still held the greater part of the country;

and if the annihilation of the Creoles came within the calculations of some of the Spanish chiefs, the object of the Venezuelan leaders was to found a homeland and increase the population and wealth. So that when they put themselves on the level of the savage irregular commanders who won the country back for the Spaniards, they really put back the hour of independence. Bolívar soon realized that the *guerra a muerte* was indefensible, politically as well as morally. He attempted to palliate its effects; but was not able to stop it until 1816.

At the beginning Bolívar's raid into Venezuela was a triumphant success. He set out with only six hundred men and five field-guns; but by a series of brilliant military movements, catching the enemy in small, isolated forces and destroying them one by one before they had time to unite against him, he paralysed Royalist resistance. He left Cúcuta, near the frontier of New Granada, on 13th May, 1813, and by 6th August he was in Caracas; the Venezuelan provinces of Mérida, Trujillo and Caracas were free once more. Arismendi had recovered the island of Margarita; while Mariño, Bermúdez, Piar and Sucre had set out from Trinidad in January, and by August had regained Maturín and Cumaná.

In Caracas, Bolívar established what was in fact a dictatorship, though he had to give it an appearance of legality to gain the support of those who still dreamt of reviving the constitutional regime of 1811 before the war was over. He could not relinquish his hold on authority, for he regarded it as absolutely necessary for carrying on the war; and in fact both legislative and executive functions rested with the commander of the liberating army. He had to leave Caracas almost at once, to take charge of operations against Puerto Cabello. He captured one of the Spanish irregular leaders, but offered to exchange him, with four other Royalist prisoners, for a Republican colonel. Monteverde's reply was a curt refusal, adding that in future, for every Spaniard sacrificed, he would shoot two Spanish Americans. Bolívar hanged the Royalist leader Zuazola—he was one of the greatest scoundrels of his time—but persisted in his attempts to exchange other prisoners, offering two Spaniards for every Spanish American. Monteverde refused, and shot four Republican officers.

On 14th October, 1813, the municipality of Caracas, in extraordinary session, and in open council (*cabildo abierto*) acclaimed Bolívar Captain-General of the patriot forces and conferred upon him the title of Liberator, *Libertador*. It was the one title which Bolívar always valued, the only one he liked to hear and to use, though he declared that the real liberators were the officers and men of the liberating army. It was not military despotism, he said, in returning thanks, that made for the welfare of a people; nor was the command with which he had been invested ever suited to a republic, except in moments of emergency. A successful soldier has no right to command his country. He was not the arbiter of its laws and administration, but the defender of its liberties. He begged them to relieve him from a load heavier than he could bear. The idea that he might resign was not taken seriously then; indeed it would have been criminal for him to do so. Later in life he showed that he was really capable of resigning the highest position in the State. For the present, he accepted the dictatorship until elections could be held.

But Venezuela was about to be lost once more. This time is was not due to delay or loss of heart of the army commander. Bolívar was of a very different temper from Miranda; and when he made mistakes, it was through daring or impulsiveness. The Spaniards had found the most useful allies in the class of *pardos* or *mestizos* (browns or half-breeds). Brown men, too, formed the greater part of the Royalist cavalry of Boves, and they ended by destroying the Second Venezuelan Republic. Boves was of Spanish birth, a smuggler by profession. His real name was Rodríguez; but he had changed it to Boves in gratitude to a firm of traders, which had once employed him, and got him out of a sentence of penal servitude. He had joined the Republicans at first; but went over to the Royalists. He had made himself at home with the semi-savage *llaneros* ("plainsmen"): wild, half-naked cowboys of the hot plains; lawless, submitting to no one; superb horsemen, and dreaded by their enemies (and particularly by their prisoners) for their fearful efficiency with the lance. It was all the same to them, whether they fought for a king or followed an outcast like Boves, or rode (as they did afterwards with Páez) for an independent republic. The words "king," "republic," "independence" meant nothing to them, for all they knew was their own freedom—freedom from all possible restraints.

Over the grass, the palm tree;
Over the palm, the sky;
Over my horse—I;
And over *I*, my sombrero.

So runs a *llanero* song, and in their peaceful moments the *llaneros* were musicians and dancers. They sang their *coplas*, their verses, to a *bandola* (mandoline), guitar or rattle (*maraca*); or they danced the wild, whirling *joropo* with a brown companion—a *samba* (the feminine counterpart of a *sambo*), who combined the physical and mental qualities of a negro and an Indian with the grace and passion of a Spanish dancer.

Boves made himself chief of a band of men like that; and as long as the *llaneros* were against it the Republic had no chance. In February 1814 he fell upon a Republican force of 3,000 with 7,000 of his lancers, and overwhelmed them. Hardly a Republican lived to tell the tale, and in future no Republican force could stand against him; whenever a town or village was occupied the inhabitants were massacred by *llanero* lancers. Boves deliberately aimed at exterminating the Creoles, thus depriving the country of the best elements of the population.

The new Spanish Captain-General, Don Juan Manuel Cajigal, a humane and civilized man, was nauseated by what he found being done in the name of Spain, and reported in that sense to the government at home. Bolívar rushed from one point of danger to another, in a vain endeavour to stop the frightful massacres of Boves, while the British governor of Curaçao badgered him about the treatment of Royalist prisoners. Bolívar answered tartly that clemency had not had the desired result; prisoners granted passports to leave the country returned to fight again for the Royalists, and the atrocities of the enemy obliged him to take reprisals. There is no record of the British governor ever having protested to Boves.

By February 1814 Boves was marching towards the centre, while Rosete, another bloodthirsty bandit, was approaching Ocumare from the north-east. At La Guaira, the prisoners attempted to break out, and the commandant sent to Bolívar for instructions. Bolívar, desperate at the successes of Boves and the trail of massacre which he left everywhere behind him, replied from Valencia on 8th February. He understood the critical circumstances only too well: the small garrison, the large number of prisoners. The condition of the Commandant of La Guaira in February 1814 was like his own when he was commanding at Puerto Cabello in 1812 and the prisoners broke out and took possession of the castle. In the days before machine-guns, a few men with muskets could easily be rushed by a crowd. There was only one way out, and he had to take it. "You will execute forthwith all the Spanish prisoners confined in the vaults, without exception." Similar orders were sent to the commandant at Caracas, Colonel J. B. Arismendi. The orders were duly carried out. Over 800 Spaniards and Canary Islanders perished, though Arismendi reported that, when certain well-known citizens of Caracas made themselves responsible for the conduct of some of the persons on the list, he thought it better to spare them to avoid mistakes.

On 28th February, Boves attacked Bolívar on his own estate at San Mateo, where he had his headquarters. His gardens and plantations were trampled under foot; his house, outbuildings and stables were shot to pieces. The ammunition dump was a building called *El Ingenio*, the sugar mill or engine-house, and was defended by the Colombian Captain Ricaurte, who had followed Bolívar from New Granada. Seeing an overwhelming attack developing at that point, Ricaurte ordered his men to retire, and then blew up the house, the ammunition and himself, just when the enemy had broken in. *El Ingenio* has remained a ruin, just as it was in 1814; but no Colombian or Venezuelan will pass it to-day without a salute to the memory of Ricaurte.

By this time fresh Spanish troops were beginning to reach Venezuela from Spain. The Peninsular War was over, and they were no longer needed in Europe. Bolívar succeeded in defeating some of them under the Captain-General at Carabobo (the first battle at that place) on 28th May; but Boves, with 5,000 lancers and 3,000 infantry, caught Bolívar and Mariño at La Puerta on 15th June with only 2,300 men, and the Republicans were utterly defeated; more than half of them were left dead on the field, including Bolívar's two secretaries, and all the prisoners were speared or shot. Bolívar got back to Caracas by the skin of his teeth. Valencia held out from 9th June to 9th July, only surrendering when food and ammunition were at an end; Boves failed to keep the terms, and soldiers and civilians were lanced or knifed without mercy. He gave a dance, which all the women were ordered to attend; meanwhile their menfolk were rounded-up in a field and "lanced as if they had been bulls." Boves stood in the ball-room with a whip in his hand. The clatter of horses' hooves on the cobbles outside made the women fear that something was wrong; but Boves cracked his whip and made them dance the *piquirico* and other dances of the country. It is said that he gave quarter to no man, unless he were a musician or a surgeon.

On 6th July Bolívar evacuated Caracas. Many of the inhabitants preferred to follow him, rather than wait for Boves; and he was accompanied by something like 10,000 men, women and children on the long retreat of 150 miles to Barcelona in the hot country near the coast; "a long tale of people of all conditions and all ages, fleeing in terror on foot, and carrying whatever they could." Many perished on the journey, from privations which can hardly be imagined. "Of the 40,000 souls which had formed the population of the Venezuelan capital—before the earthquake—there remained now only the nuns of the Conception and the Carmen, a few friars, the archbishop and the canons of the cathedral, with 4,000 or 5,000 persons who preferred to await death in their own homes rather than expose themselves to the even greater risks of flight." At the end of three months, wandering in the wilds, those who had been able to reach Cumaná (250 miles east of Caracas) were gradually embarked for the Island of Margarita and the British West Indies.

The advance guard of the Royalist army entered Caracas two days after the pitiful pilgrimage had left it. The commander lost no time in proclaiming an amnesty, and the proclamation was repeated by Boves when he arrived a week later. But those patriots who ventured to come out of hiding were either taken outside the city and shot, or removed to Calabozo and shot there.

Bolívar attempted to make a stand at Aragua de Barcelona, 60 miles from Barcelona itself, with 3,000 men. But on 18th August he was attacked by 8,000 under Morales, and finally defeated. Morales cut the throats not only of all the prisoners but also of a great part of the inhabitants and a large number of refugees. He spared neither age nor sex, carrying his massacre (as Rosete had done) into the parish church, where more than a thousand people were killed.

Bolívar eventually reached the port of Cumaná. He was told that the Italian commander of the few vessels which belonged to the Republic was making off with what little treasure they still possessed. Bolívar and Mariño followed him round the point, to Margarita Island, where they succeeded in persuading him to hand over two ships, with two-thirds of the silver, to the authorities on the Island. The Italian kept the other third for his "expenses." It was not a good bargain, but it enabled Margarita Island to hold on for some time, in quasi-independence. On their return to the mainland, Bolívar found that the officers on shore had deprived him of his command, alleging that the journey to the island had been attempted desertion. The conditions were not unlike those at La Guaira in 1812, when Bolívar had arrested Miranda. On this occasion, however, they were able to justify themselves enough to be allowed to embark for the West Indies.

Boves occupied Cumaná on 16th October, cutting the throats of prisoners, women and children. On 5th December he defeated the remaining Republican leaders, but lost his own life. Meanwhile his lieutenant, Morales, drove the remaining Republicans to Maturín, near the delta of the Orinoco, where the usual massacre took place once more. By the end of 1814, the Republicans held only Margarita Island; while a few leaders, such as Páez, were still in existence on the mainland with scattered guerrilla bands, in remote and inaccessible places.

A Spanish official wrote: "There are no more provinces left. Towns which had thousands of inhabitants are now reduced to a few hundreds or even a few dozen. Of others, there are nothing but vestiges, to show that they were once inhabited by human beings. Roads and fields are full of unburied corpses; whole villages have been burnt; whole families are nothing but a memory. . . . Agriculture has stopped, and in the towns they are short of the most essential articles of food."

The irony of it was that many people in Venezuela had not wanted independence, least of all the brown half-breeds. The revolution had been made by the white Creoles like Bolívar, and it was they who had been the first and greatest sufferers. Entire families had been wiped out, and those persons who had not lost their lives had lost everything else. Bolívar's friend—his wife's uncle—the Marqués del Toro, was working as a jobbing gardener at Port of Spain, Trinidad; and he was lucky. His brother, Fernando, was hobbling about on a wooden leg. Most of their set had been shot or hanged or lanced. Those left alive were (as one of them put it) "poor as Christ, stricken with fever, with one foot in prison and the other in exile." "My relations," another survivor wrote to Bolívar, "and that enchanting girl you will not have forgotten, are enjoying heaven now, thanks to Boves. . . . My mother is dead, but I am alive—no doubt for some good purpose."

That was what war meant in Venezuela.

Chapter Five

From Jamaica to Angostura: Political Thought

THE Spanish expedition of 15,000 men, which reached Venezuela in April 1815, had originally been intended for the River Plate. Fortunately for those provinces, its destination was changed, and Venezuela had to bear the full weight of the Spanish blow for reconquest.

Arismendi handed over the Isle of Margarita under an amnesty which the new Spanish commander faithfully observed. General Morillo, though severe and uncompromising, was a soldier who had risen from the ranks. He knew how to obey orders, and was of a different stamp from the bandit and cut-throat leaders who had won back the country for the Royalists. Yet his dispositions in Caracas were harsh, and his orders were passed on in the style of Boves. "You will omit all humane consideration," a subordinate was informed. "All insurgents, or those who followed them, with arms or without; those who have assisted them in the past and may assist them in the future . . . will be shot without reprieve, and without any written *proceso* or *sumario.*" Suspects were to have no more than a brief, verbal trial before two or three officers.

Meanwhile Bolívar, rejected by his own subordinates in September 1814, returned to Cartagena and went up to Tunja where the Confederate Congress of New Granada was sitting. His report on the expedition to Venezuela was accepted; and though it had ended in disaster, he was given another command. This time he had to deal with a group of insurgents, representing certain provinces of New Granada which already desired to secede from the new republic. On his way up to Tunja he had been joined by some troops which General Urdaneta—a loyal officer and devoted adherent—had saved from capture in western Venezuela, and had led into New Granada by way of Cúcuta. He could therefore offer the Congress at Tunja a small force of seasoned troops, and he soon reduced the rebellious garrison at Santa Fe de Bogotá. Promoted "Captain-General of the armies of the Confederation," he was given a further 2,000 men, to free the coastal provinces of Santa Marta and Maracaibo from the Royalists; but the local commander at Cartagena, Colonel Castillo, refused to let Bolívar in; and for three months kept him waiting outside the town. Castillo was a personal enemy of Bolívar, and had an old grievance against him: Bolívar had been appointed over his head to command the expedition into Venezuela which had led to the capture of Caracas, and Castillo refused to hand over the munitions and supplies which, on instructions from Santa Fe, should have enabled the expedition to reach Santa Marta.

Bolívar tried every means of conciliation. At last, to avoid something like civil war, he resigned his command. On 23rd July, 1815, Morillo and Morales reached Santa Marta, and on 1st September they besieged Castillo in Cartagena. After six weeks, the garrison refused to obey Castillo any longer, and on the 6th, the Royalists made their entry. They shot 3 officers, 60 men and 300 civilians; Castillo was tried by court martial and hanged. Morillo went up to Santa Fe de Bogotá and behaved in the same manner, 60 civilians being shot out of hand. The Independent Confederation of New Granada ceased to exist. It had suffered much less than the Republic of Venezuela, but it disappeared in much the same way: drowned in blood.

Bolívar meanwhile was in Jamaica, waiting for the opportunity of going on with the war of independence. It was not that he never knew when he was beaten. He knew only too well. He had been beaten twice, thoroughly, and should have been utterly discredited. But one of his greatest qualities was that he was always ready to try again. From Jamaica (6th September, 1815) he wrote a long letter to an English correspondent who had asked his opinion on the future of the Spanish American peoples. The inquirer is supposed to have been the Duke of Manchester, at that time governor of Jamaica, a man of wide human sympathy and considerable political intelligence.

Bolívar must have realized by this time that there were two main types of Englishmen influential in foreign policy and foreign relations: the types represented respectively by Canning and Byron. If Canning did great things for British power and influence and trade—and, with these objects in view, materially discouraged Spain from persisting in the reconquest of South America—Byron did as much or more to establish Britain in the eyes of all nations as the great paladin of justice and liberty; and the legend, though tarnished in European eyes by the South African war, lived on until the time of Munich, and came to life again after the events of 1940 and 1941. Yet the Englishman whom most foreign peoples admire is still the "mad" Englishman, the eccentric idealist, rather than the clear-sighted statesman or the hard-headed man of business. "By nothing is England so great as in her poetry." To many people abroad, Byron is still the ideal Englishman, because of his eccentricities no less than because of his poetry; to the Spanish novelist Pío Baroja, there is nothing more English than a romantic poet who could yet be punctual and business-like, and organize an expeditionary force for a war of liberation. Bolívar understood both temperaments, Canning's and Byron's; and though his own was closer to

Byron's, he had a strong enough will to make himself the Canning of his own country and its Byron as well. Byron, for his part, knew that he had something in common with Bolívar. From his letters we learn that in 1822 he had a boat called the *Bolívar*, and that in 1819 he made several inquiries in London as to the possibility of emigrating to South America and settling in Venezuela, "Bolívar's country." [1] "I should not make a bad South American planter," he wrote, "and I should take my natural daughter, Allegra, with me, and settle." Bolívar, the romantic man of action, was a Byron who discovered—earlier than Byron himself—that his life's work was to be a liberator.

When Bolívar sat down to answer the Duke of Manchester's letter, he wrote a reply such as Byron might have written on the absurdity of Turkey continuing to hold Greece. What madness it was, he exclaimed, for Spain to try to reconquer South America without sea-power, without credit, and almost without armed forces! Such armed forces as it had were hardly enough to keep its own people in a state of forced obedience, let alone to defend it from its neighbours. Could that nation monopolize the trade of half the world without manufactures of its own, without products of the soil, without technical efficiency or scientific knowledge? Europe would do Spain a real service by dissuading her from

[1] This was pointed out to me by the Spanish poet Luis Cernuda.

such rash and obstinate behaviour. The idea of South American independence should have originated in Europe; a sound European policy would have called the independent states of America into existence both because the balance of the world demanded it (Bolívar anticipated a famous phrase of Canning's), and because that was the only certain and legitimate method by which European states could obtain commercial establishments overseas.

As in the great speech at the opening of the Congress at Angostura (which came later) Bolívar compared the actual condition of America to that of Europe on the fall of the Roman Empire, each dismembered province forming a political system of its own, with some of its former traditions; but there was this difference: the Spanish-speaking Americans hardly preserved any vestiges of what had existed in ancient times. Yet, now that they had set up house for themselves, events had proved that representative institutions were not well suited to their character, or customs, or present level of intelligence. In Caracas, it had been the excess of party spirit, originating in the patriotic debating societies and popular elections, which had been responsible for bringing them back to slavery. He was not in favour of the federal system. A federal republic, like that of the United States, demanded political virtues greatly in excess of anything they had in South America; and with clear vision, he went on to predict the kind of future which seemed to be in store for the various Spanish-speaking dominions. Mexico, he thought, would have either a monarchy, supported by a military or aristocratic party (as it had afterwards with Itúrbide and Maximilian), or a life-presidency (Porfirio Díaz). The states of Central America, he hoped, would form a confederation; while canals cut through the Isthmus would shorten the distances and increase the commercial relations between Europe, America and Asia. In Buenos Aires the military party would be predominant, until they established an oligarchy or "monocracy." Chile, through its geographical position and the nature of its inhabitants, would make little alteration in its laws, and would preserve its uniformity in political and religious opinions; it would be the most stable of the Spanish American republics—a prophecy which has been confirmed by the experience of a hundred years. Peru, on the contrary, contained elements which were incompatible with a just and liberal administration: wealth and slavery. There would be violent conflict, he foresaw, between the aspirations of the rich and what he might call the "tumultuous democracy" of the freedmen and slaves. Bolívar was to have a closer acquaintance with these conditions ten years later, when he became head of the Peruvian Government. New Granada he saw united with Venezuela to form a large, centralized republic, the capital of which might be a new city—called Las Casas, after the Apostle of the Indies—on the border between the two states. The new republic would be called Colombia; and its form of government might imitate that of England, with a hereditary Upper House, and a Lower House elected by popular vote. Instead of a king, there would be a president—perhaps elected for life, but in no case able to pass on the succession to his son. Finally, he suggested to his English correspondent the idea of an international congress of the new States, meeting at Panamá to discuss questions of war and peace with the other nations of the world.

These ideas, and above all the last two, were the long dream of the Liberator's life, and the source of many of his sorrows. But now, in 1815, he was dreaming them as an exile in a foreign colony, with no money, no arms and no ships; while his own land was once again a conquered country, with the enemy in occupation. His own life, too, was in danger; he narrowly escaped being murdered by a Negro—in the pay (it is believed) of his political enemies—and only escaped by suddenly and unexpectedly changing his lodgings. A friend who was expecting him, and had gone to sleep in the hammock while he was waiting, received the death blows meant for the Liberator himself.

Jamaica seemed unlikely to provide the resources which Bolívar wanted. He moved to the Negro Republic of Haiti, where President Petion, along with a shipowner of Curaçao (Louis Brion) and a British merchant (Robert Sutherland), provided him with muskets and ammunition, ships and money. With seven schooners and 200 men, he set sail for Margarita Island, where the indomitable Arismendi, with a few hundred fishermen and peons from the plantations, had once more raised the standard of independence.

Bolívar's expedition landed on 3rd May, 1816; but after 1st July, when the patriots reached the mainland at Carúpano, they wasted time in unjustifiable dissensions. On 6th July Bolívar occupied Ocumare and declared the slaves free; it was a promise he had made to the Negroes of Haiti and their friendly President, who alone had been kind and helpful at a time when liberation had seemed hopeless. He declared, too, that there should be no more *guerra a muerte*. He began military operations by sending forward his lieutenants: MacGregor, Soublette, Torres, Briceño, Anzoátegui—all to become well-known names in the story of the reconquest—to invade the valley of Aragua, near Caracas. They began with some success; but superior Spanish forces drove them back to Ocumare. Bolívar made a sortie to help them, but the Royalists cut them off. The leaders and a few of their men rode through the Spaniards and joined the guerrilla forces which had been leading a precarious existence in the plains, and gained several small successes, including an important engagement at Juncal.

The Republicans had not done very well; dissensions among them delayed their recovery. Bolívar's chief difficulty at this time was the unreliability of some of his commanders. Mariño was unaccountable, and jealous of Bolívar. He had gone his own way against the Royalists, and had met with severe reverses. Arismendi was a good soldier, but apt to be led astray by idle talk. Sucre was firmly loyal; more intelligent, more diplomatic than the others: he was the only one who, in time to come, was to emulate his chief, not only as a leader in war but also as an administrator in peace. He negotiated with Mariño in such a way as not to make him lose patience, showing a due respect to his military seniority and his services to the cause, and making him believe that he had rendered signal service by not plunging the infant Venezuelan Republic into civil war. "To lessen the extent of an evil is in itself a good," Bolívar had said to Sucre: "and that good ought to be rewarded, so far as is compatible with the dignity of the government." That was the great difficulty in exercising clemency, he added; but if Mariño went on disobeying orders, he should be placed under arrest. Mariño submitted.

The chief cause of the trouble was the personal ascendancy of Bolívar himself. Bolívar's insistence on exercising supreme personal authority was distasteful to those who wished to see what they believed to be more real democracy and representative government; but in a state of war, and in the conditions in which they were living, Bolívar had to impose his own will on all the others. He was the only man among them who had a clear vision, both of the military present and of the political future. Bolívar's mind had been largely formed by writers of the Age of Reason. He saw things as they were; and at the moment, in the state of emergency in which the patriots found themselves, government by discussion was unworkable. The other leaders wanted democratic institutions at once; they could not understand, or accept, the idea of democratic rule achieved by undemocratic means. Bolívar's secretary, who was attached for a time to Piar, wrote: "They do not want to do the least thing against you; your authority is respected, and still exists. All they want is to give you a senate or council, so that the form of government may have a semblance of democracy and representation. It is a measure more important to yourself, than to anyone else; for, with your supreme authority, you can do what you like without limit, while they, with their insignificant project, can lull the others to sleep." General Piar went farther than Mariño; his disobedience to orders became disloyalty, his disloyalty treachery; he was court-martialled and shot. Bolívar was most reluctant to take this step; and only did so as a warning to others. Piar was a capable guerrilla leader, but he was incapable of obeying orders; at the very moment when Bolívar was anxious to put a stop to the *guerra a muerte*, he had shot between 160 and 300 Royalist prisoners. Piar had also occupied the Catalan missions at Caroní; and the monks who were brought away by two officers and a party of Indians, in the direction of a village called Divina Pastora, were never heard of again. Then he had been trying to stir up racial antagonism, dividing the brown *pardos* from the white Creoles represented by Bolívar. Piar's own origin is uncertain, though he always liked to be taken for a Creole himself, and the real question settled by his execution was the power of a divisional general against the commander-in-chief. If Bolívar had not acted when he did Piar would have risen against him with the victorious guerrillas in Guiana, producing anarchy and an end to all the patriot hopes against the Spaniards.

Bolívar, with his blend of audacity and serenity, was the only man who could save the new republic from disaster. Piar and Mariño could command in the field, in a limited sphere of action; but they had nothing like the strategic sense, or interest in the larger plans, needed for an extended campaign. Neither Arismendi nor Bermúdez was particularly clever; but they had the impetuous courage which won positions from the enemy, while most of the others, including Páez, the greatest, were leaders of guerrillas.

Páez was a *mestizo*, and inclined to dislike Creoles like Bolívar who came from *familias mantuanas*. He was born in 1790 near Acarigua in the Venezuelan province of Barinas; his father was a travelling tobacconist and the boy had very little schooling. The schoolmistress he mentions in his *Memoirs* taught him to read—very badly—a book of *doctrina cristiana* which the boys had to learn by heart or have it knocked into them with a stick. His cousin took him away from school early, to serve in the shop and spend early morning and evening in the fields, sowing *cacao*. At 17 he went to the *llanos*, the great grassy river-plains, where he lived as a cowboy till he could become a cattle-dealer on his own. To his experience of cowboy life he owed the authority which he afterwards had over the bands of *llanero* roughriders and also the habit of watchfulness and suspicion which, after the death of Bolívar in 1830, helped him to turn into the astute politician he became in later life. He joined the patriot forces in 1810. In 1812, when the Spaniards had recovered their hold on the country, he retired with the rank of sergeant. In 1814, he joined up again, in the fighting on the plains of the Apure; and went on from success to success, until on the field of Carabobo Bolívar promoted him major-general. He was of medium height, broad-shouldered, thick-lipped and round-headed. According to O'Leary, he was subject to epileptic fits; the least contradiction produced convulsions which left him senseless. But as a guerrilla-leader, he was unequalled; the fewer the men he had, the more successful he was.

In 1816 Páez might have been described as a commander of allied troops, acting independently. By 1818, Bolívar had incorporated him in his own forces, together with the horsemen which Páez had commanded in the plains. Compared with the Spanish forces under Morillo—disciplined regular troops, many of whom had been through the war against Napoleon—Bolívar had only a few ill-trained *guerrilleros*, or partisans, holding the remote and inaccessible east end of the country. But he realized that, if he could occupy certain points, the future might be his. He proceeded systematically, in spite of his small numbers, and the doubtful loyalty of some of his lieutenants, clearing Royalist ships off the Orinoco, and blockading the Venezuelan part of Guiana. This was accomplished after three months of manœuvring and fighting on the wet river plains: night-surprises and hair-breadth escapes, such as the affair at Casacoima, when Bolívar and his staff came as near as possible to being captured by the Spaniards. At last, on 17th July, 1816, the Royalists evacuated Angostura, and on 3rd August they abandoned all the positions which they held in Venezuelan Guiana.

Angostura (now called Ciudad Bolívar) is on

the south bank of the Orinoco, about 270 miles from the Delta, and about 600 miles, in a direct line, from Caracas. It is the trading centre for all that part of Venezuela; the river there is about a mile broad, and on the opposite bank is the small town of Soledad. Bolívar was now in control of the lower Orinoco and its banks, with Páez and his *llanero* cavalry harrying Morillo's Spaniards, and he saw that with any luck the future was safe. He wrote confidently to the Marqués del Toro, still gardening in Trinidad, explaining his plans.

> "This province [of Guiana] is a key-point. From here, we shall take the enemy in the rear all the way to Santa Fe. We have an immense territory on both banks of the Orinoco, Apure, Meta and Arauca; we have all the cattle and horses we want, and all we have to do is to hold our ground and prolong the campaign. The side which makes the most of this advantage will win."

The Spanish commander had about 14,000 men in Venezuela. Bolívar planned to get round them, through the almost impassable *llanos*, and cross the Andes into New Granada where the Viceroy had a much smaller force, and defeat that.

In some ways, at this moment, independence seemed farther off than ever. The Royalists were still in complete control of the west and centre; while in the east, though it was mainly held by Bolívar and his Republicans, there were, still, endless bickerings and disagreements among the local commanders. Arismendi, on Margarita Island, was behaving like a semi-independent feudal lord; and Páez, on the Apure, was never quite above the suspicion of intrigue. Yet this was the moment when Bolívar's head was clearer than ever. His plans for the future began to take definite shape: he would summon a parliament at Angostura, establish a constitutional government, and then march up the Orinoco and its tributary the Apure, cross the Andes, and invade New Granada behind the backs of the Spaniards.

Some writers have raised their eyebrows at Bolívar's "absurd notion" of summoning a parliament, when he had hardly a capital, let alone a country, to call his own; and only two Venezuelan provinces were completely free to send representatives to the congress of the Venezuelan nation. Yet from the moment when he had established his capital in that sleepy riverside town in the tropics, summoned a parliament, and opened it with a lecture on political philosophy, his luck turned and his star began to rise. That eloquent academic discourse at Angostura, with its references to Greece and Rome, France and England—Plutarch, Locke, Montesquieu and Rousseau—was the prelude to the crossing of the Andes, the liberation of New Granada, Venezuela, Quito and Peru, and the foundation of an entirely new State which the inhabitants named after its Liberator: Bolivia.

The Liberator knew very well what he was about. When it became known abroad that Angostura and the Orinoco provinces had fallen, the cause of independence recovered its good name, more especially in Britain and the United States—the countries from which Bolívar could expect both moral and material support. In London, López Méndez, the Venezuelan agent, was now able to organize volunteers, float loans, and send consignments of arms and equipment. In the United States, the agent was not so successful; but President Monroe informed Congress that the war in Venezuela was now to be regarded as a civil war between contending parties with equal rights to be considered belligerents. Bolívar knew how important it was to show the world that free Venezuela had a real government and a democratic constitution, and did not support itself entirely by feats of arms.

The Liberator was joined by something very like the International Brigade of the Spanish Civil War. The British contingent was by far the largest; fighting as a separate unit, it saved the situation for Bolívar at one or two very awkward and dangerous moments, while his English brigaders marched all over Venezuela bawling the tune of *Ye gentlemen of England*—sometimes with rather peculiar words. Comparatively few of the British Legion ever got back to their own country.

Bolívar, who had made himself into an army

commander through sheer force of character and strength of will, never forgot his own men, and, for that, they adored him. Again, for all his quickness and his gift for improvisation, he never neglected to make the most thorough preparations that time allowed. Compared with the thorough professional, military dispositions made by San Martín to cross the Andes and liberate Chile, Bolívar's preparations seem curiously inadequate. Yet he could hardly have done more. San Martín had all the time he wanted and a friendly government to back him in Buenos Aires, while Bolívar had to see to every detail himself. His letters and papers about this date are full of such things as the exact pattern of horseshoe he wanted, the particular quality of soft iron to be used in making them; the quantities and transport of ammunition and the number and destination of *damajuanas* (demijohns) of black powder. From July to September he was busy distributing equipment and stores; and he travelled from one end of the liberated provinces to the other—from Maturín in the east to the Apure in the west—keeping an eye on everything that concerned the army of liberation. On 8th February, 1819, he was back at Angostura; and on the 15th he attended the opening of the new Congress.

His "Message" is a most remarkable document; not only a speech for the opening of a parliament, but a dissertation on the political philosophy of

Spanish-speaking America; and it stands with the Memorial written at Cartagena, the Letter from Jamaica, and the Constitution of Bolivia, among the Liberator's greatest pronouncements. Bolívar dictated it during a journey to the Apure, between 21st December, 1818, and 8th February, 1819, and sent the rough draft to Manuel Palacio Fajardo, one of the signatories of the Venezuelan Declaration of Independence in 1811. Palacio deleted one or two sentences and removed one or two repetitions; but he admired the speech greatly, and spoke warmly of the translation made by one of Bolívar's English friends.

From the discourse at Angostura, as from the earlier letter from Jamaica and the later Constitution for Bolivia, we may see how deeply Bolívar was affected by the political thought of both France and England. He had read widely in the works of the French *philosophes* and their successors: Voltaire, Montesquieu, Rousseau, Helvétius, Raynal and others, including Volney. We know too that he was influenced by English political thinkers, chiefly Locke; but it is clear that while French influence directed his theory, English example controlled his practice. At first the French influence predominated. Bolívar was a liberal republican, and his definition of the rights of man—the liberty of acting, thinking, speaking and writing—is an echo of the doctrine which inspired the French Revolution. In theory his ideal state was a republic based on political equality, though taking account of the physical and moral inequalities considered in Rousseau's *Discours sur l'inégalité.* But when it came to practice, and he was faced by the actual conditions in South America, he realized that his countrymen were not yet sufficiently advanced, either in education or in a sense of political responsibility. With their "inheritance of slavery," as it was called, how could they be fit for the privileges which a democratic government conferred on them? The federal system of the United States, inspiring though it was, proved ill-adapted to Venezuela. Federal government, as it was understood in South America, only led to disunion, while what was wanted was unity, particularly at so crucial a stage in the development of a new country. Montesquieu had seen that, and he had taught Bolívar the futility of imitating the federal system of the North; laws and institutions should be adapted to the country for which they were intended. Like Rousseau, Bolívar understood the importance of education —of educating people so that they might be fitted for the democratic way of life; but in the meantime he had to provide a government more suited to their capacities than the federal system of the United States: a confederation of the different Venezuelan districts into one strong united State, with powerful executive officials and a hereditary senate. He also insisted on the separation of the executive and legislative powers. But, in most respects, his model was the Constitution of Great Britain; and there is an unmistakable likeness between the powers of Bolívar's president and those of an English constitutional monarch. The conception probably came to him from Montesquieu, but the idea was originally English.

Bolívar began his speech at Angostura with a historical summary. The origins of their present situation, he said, could be found in the records of Spanish rule in America, in the Laws of the Indies, in the acts of the various Viceroys and Spanish governors. The Church, too, had played its part in maintaining the colonies in bondage to the mother country; and all of these causes should be considered in attempting to account for the brusque action of the Republican Government in proclaiming its independence of Spain, and for the ferocity of the supporters of Spain in opposing it. The separation of South America from the Spanish monarchy resembled nothing so much as the Roman Empire falling to pieces at the beginning of the Dark Ages. The dismembered parts of the Empire formed independent peoples; but in Europe those peoples returned to a certain extent to their original condition, while in Venezuela they had left hardly a vestige of what they were before the Spaniards came. The present inhabitants of Venezuela were neither Europeans nor Indians, but an intermediate race between the two. They were Europeans by rights, but Americans by birth, and they were placed in the extraordinary predicament of having to dispute their title to possession of their own country with the original inhabitants, and of having at the same time to maintain themselves in the country of their birth against the Spanish invaders. So far they had been purely passive, their political existence had been nil, and they had had great difficulty in establishing their liberties. South America had received everything from Spain; but it had never been allowed to manage its own affairs, and the inhabitants had been kept completely out of the world in everything concerned with government.

What kind of government ought they to have? There were, he went on, many systems of government, but most of them were really systems of oppression. The whole earth had been, and largely still was, the victim of its governments. Men were endowed by nature with "an inclination to liberty"; but whether from sloth, or some other cause, their liberty was still restricted, and it was true, if humiliating, that it was more difficult for a people to preserve a just balance of liberty than to put up with a load of tyranny. Democracy alone was compatible with complete liberty; the difficulty was that no democratic government had ever possessed at the same time power, prosperity and permanence, while aristocracy and monarchy had established great and powerful empires. So far Bolívar had been speaking as the disciple of Rousseau.

In the Republic of Venezuela, he continued, they had abolished monarchy, class-distinction and privilege; they had declared the Rights of Man: the liberty of acting, thinking, speaking and writing. Their constitution was a federal republic. But the federal republic, he thought, was a mistake. The more he admired the good points of a federal system, the more convinced he became of the impossibility of applying it to their own situation. And, of course, it hardly applied to their situation at all. Federalism, strictly speaking, is the voluntary union of independent states; the great examples are Switzerland, the Netherlands, and the United States of North America. But in South America, federalism in practice meant not union but disunion: the looser union and independent action of provinces which had formerly been united firmly and governed centrally. Montesquieu believed that federalism arose from the sparseness of the population, which left no adequate means of defence against the encroachment of foreign monarchies; it was a system which solved the problem of providing the necessary measure of self-defence without loss of republican spirit (*Esprit des lois*, IX, i). Otherwise, he held that republican government was only appropriate to small territories, while monarchy was suited to territories of moderate size, and despotism to the more extensive regions (*Esprit des lois*, VIII, xvi).

South Americans had taken the United States for their model; but the success of the United States had blinded them to the real nature of federalism. North American writings on the subject, the essays published as *The Federalist*, in 1787 and 1788, were not translated into Spanish until long after (1868 and 1887), though their substance became known in a Spanish form in the writings of Vicente Rocafuerte, an Ecuadorian, who published various books between 1822 and 1826 explaining in simple language what the advantages of federalism were likely to be. Bolívar knew *The Federalist*, but he did not at first distinguish clearly between the two kinds of federalism, though he saw that in the South America of his day what was understood by federalism would not work. All through his career, his aim was to unite American states, not divide them. It was extraordinary, he thought, that a system which seemed so weak and complicated should be able to exist, even in the former British colonies. It has been a mistake to copy it in Venezuela; to think that two nations, so distinct as the Anglo-American and Spanish-American, could do the same thing. Again he quoted Montesquieu: laws should be suited to the people using them; they should depend on the physical state of the country, climate, soil, geographical position and extent; on the way of life of the inhabitants, the amount of liberty they could stand, their economic condition, commerce, manners and customs. That was the code they ought to consult, rather than any pronouncement of George Washington. He advised his audience at Angostura to read the history of Spain and the Laws of the Indies, the past and present of South America. They would find that climatic conditions had a direct connexion with the difference between one population and another; and institutions must necessarily vary according to the characteristics of the people. It would be difficult to apply to Spain the political, civil and religious practices of Britain; and it would be even more difficult to apply to Venezuela the constitutional practice of the United States. The truth was that in Venezuela they were not ready for a completely representative system; and in deciding on the federal form of administration, they had acted in deference to the feelings of the different provinces, rather than laying the solid foundations of a strong, centralized state. For a government of that kind, Venezuela lacked the necessary preparation.

By the Venezuelan constitution, all citizens were entitled to political liberty. The idea that all men are born with equal rights to the benefits of society was well known. Bolívar did not mention Roman Law; but the theory is stated by the Roman jurist Ulpian: *Cum jure naturali omnes liberi nascerentur*, "By natural law all are born free"; and it is included in the Virginia Bill of Rights (1776) in the postulate "that all men are by nature equally free." The idea that all men are *created* equal is different; it came into American revolutionary thought through Luther and Calvin. But the theory that all men are born with equal rights had, as Bolívar said, already been sanctioned by thinkers in other ages. Yet not all men are born with equal capacity. Nature made men unequal in genius, in temperament, in strength and in character; but laws corrected that difference, while education, industry, arts and sciences gave them political and social equality. In Venezuela, in particular, their diversity of origin needed the most careful attention; their hands, he put it, were free, but their hearts were still numbed by the effects of servitude. Their future depended on what they made of their new Constitution. Above all, their government must be stable; but to achieve that, there would have to be a strong public opinion.

Government, Bolívar insisted, should be based on the sovereignty of the people. He had read Plutarch and pointed to Athens: a brilliant example of absolute democracy, but at the same time a melancholy proof of the weakness of that kind of government. Solon (in 594 B.C.), the wisest legislator in Greece, hardly saw his republic last ten years, and had to admit that it was inadequate. He had shown how difficult it was to govern men by simple laws; and only later, under an absolutist government, had Athens enjoyed her greatest prosperity, with laws that were mild, wise and politic. Pisistratus, the usurper and a tyrant of thirty years later, did more good to Athens, he thought, than her laws; Pericles, though a usurper too, was a great and useful citizen. He reminded them that the Republic of Sparta, which seemed so fantastic an institution —a republic with two kings—produced more real effects than the ingenious world of Solon at Athens, and the legislation of Lycurgus produced glory, happiness and political virtue. Actually it is doubtful whether Lycurgus ever existed, whether he lived in the ninth century B.C. or the seventh, and whether any of the laws attributed to him were really his. Bolívar himself might be regarded as an example of the perfect legislator imagined by Rousseau: the idealized version of Lycurgus, who can force his fellow-citizens to accept a form of society, though they cannot themselves see that it is in accordance with their own "general will" (*Contrat Social*, II, vii). The Roman constitution had produced the greatest power and prosperity of any people on earth. Yet it seemed confused in form and there was no distribution of power. The consuls, the Senate and the people were all legislators, magistrates and judges, for they all participated in all of these offices; and the arrangement by which the executive consisted of two consuls had the same inconvenience as the Republic of Sparta with its two kings. Yet the

Roman Republic, a government "monstrous in form and purely warlike in intention," Bolívar said, "made the whole world a Roman Empire and proved to all men the power of political virtue."

It is typical of the age in which Bolívar lived that he should base his political philosophy on an idealized, traditional version of Greek and Roman history. On the whole, the speech at Angostura shows a certain disillusion with the ideas in which he had been brought up; but it is characteristic of him to use Greek and Roman history to justify his departure from the pure gospel of Rousseau.

Coming down to modern times he found in England and France impressive lessons in every kind of government. The revolutions in those countries had, he said, filled the world with political light. Every thinking being had learnt what were the rights and duties of man, and what constituted good government; every inquirer could assess at their proper value the speculations of modern political thinkers and legislators. The political history of England and France had, he declared, excited even "the apathetic Spaniards," who, as he put it, after becoming involved in the political whirlwind, had given ephemeral proofs of liberty—he meant the Cortes of Cadiz—but had shown their incapacity for living under the rule of law by returning to the immemorial dungeons and fires of the Inquisition. That was a criticism of the rulers of Spain, rather than of the Spanish people; but it enabled him to make the point which he quoted from memory and attributed to Volney, that the errors and misfortunes of the Old World should teach wisdom and happiness to the New.

Rome and Britain, he repeated, were the nations which had shown most talent for government, either among the ancients or the moderns. Both had learnt to command, and to be free; yet their constitutions were not modelled on any brilliant theory of liberty, but were based on solid achievement. That was why he recommended his hearers to study the British Constitution, which seemed to be the one which had the greatest possible effect on the peoples adopting it. Actually, it would make no great change in their own fundamental laws, he said, if they were to adopt a parliament like that of Great Britain; but they had followed the United States, and had divided the representatives of the nation into two houses: a Lower House chosen by popular election, and a Senate which, he thought, should be hereditary, to make sure of preserving its independence. The senators, in the first instance, would be elected by Congress, and drawn preferably from the liberators of the country: the men who had done most for the country's independence. This hereditary senate would not be a violation of political equality, he explained. It was not a nobility that he wished to establish; for that would destroy both equality and liberty.

Yet the office of senator was one for which the holders ought to be prepared. He would have them educated in a college specially set apart, so as to prepare them for the high political function which they would one day perform—an ideal as old as Plato, but one which has never yet been realized. He reminded them how valuable to the British nation the House of Lords had been; in his day it seemed to form a bulwark for popular liberties: "the Senators in Rome and the Lords in London have proved themselves the stoutest pillars of civil and political liberty." Yet Bolívar's idea of a hereditary, irresponsible Senate suggests not so much the House of Lords, as the French thinkers of the Age of Reason: the Abbé Saint-Pierre and Mably. Bolívar had been born in an age of enlightened despotism. "If ever the use of force is justified violence," Bolívar wrote to William White (26th May, 1820), "it is when employed in making men good and therefore happy. No liberty is legitimate, except when aimed at the honour of mankind and the improvement of his lot. The rest is pure illusion, and perhaps pernicious nonsense."

For the head of the state Bolívar recommended a president with powers analogous to those of the King of England; but the president, though he held office for life, was to be chosen by popular election. Bolívar insisted that the British system was the most perfect model, whether for a monarchy, an aristocracy, or a democracy; and it is interesting to find that in all his pronouncements he shows this fervent admiration for the British constitution, "for," as he put it, "its republican qualities," or those qualities in it which a republican could approve and accept.

Like Rousseau, Bolívar underlined the importance of educating as many of the inhabitants of the country as possible so that they might become fitted for democracy. But he went farther. Bolívar would borrow from Athens the idea of the Court of the Areopagus, the guardians of custom and law; from Rome, the Censors and domestic tribunals; and from Sparta, the Spartan austerity. He would give the Venezuelan Republic a fourth power, with authority to encourage public spirit, good behaviour and republican morality. It would be a new Areopagus to watch over the education of youth. This proposal for a moral power in the state, to watch over education and good behaviour, is the most curious feature of the Liberator's discourse. Miranda had proposed something of the same kind, and claimed that it would be easier to put into practice than some other schemes which had been brought in by legislators. But Bolívar widened its scope and coloured it with a memory of Greek history, making it a real political force and at the same time a practical ideal, typical of his realistic but Utopian imagination. Practicable or not, it was a characteristically Bolivarian idea: a mixture of philosophic rationalism and poetic imagination.

Bolívar was not unaware how dangerous it might be, if such a scheme fell into the wrong hands; but he was determined to make it work, so long as he had power to do so, and he introduced it into the constitution of Bolivia.

The strength of Bolívar lay in his will, fired by the force of poetic suggestion: an immanent creative power which seemed to radiate from his presence and affected all who knew him. The disproportion between the social condition of his fellow-citizens and the liberty he desired for them embittered his life and restricted the scope of his vision. So did the fact that his temper was that of a classic, formed in the Age of Reason but forced into a romantic adventure in which everything that happened was the result of unreason: *la razón de la sinrazón*, Cervantes called it. But even in moments of bitterest disillusionment in the struggle with incomprehension, treachery and ingratitude, he maintained a profoundly classical serenity, and this inspired, if it did not dominate, all his actions and all his words.

Chapter Six

Crossing the Andes

THE new constitution was discussed and passed, though at the time its importance was more theoretical than practical. On Bolívar's advice, the federal ideas of 1811 were abandoned; Venezuela was to be one and indivisible. But other parts of his plan were not accepted. There was to be no hereditary senate, or president with the powers or limitations of an English king; while the moral power, which some considered his happiest idea, was regarded by others as a moral Inquisition, hardly less damaging than the Holy Office itself. It would in any case have been very difficult to establish, and at that time was clearly impracticable. Meanwhile independence had only been regained in theory; the greater part of Venezuelan territory was still Spanish, and Bolívar's election as provisional president was only accepted by him as equivalent to that of commander of the Republican armed forces.

In order to carry through his plan of attacking the Spanish Royalists in Colombia, by-passing those in Venezuela, Bolívar had to move his forces over flooded plains in the rainy season, and across the Andes in the time of snow. In

March 1819 he reached the headquarters of Páez on the River Arauca. The Royalists and Spaniards under Morillo were barring the way at San Fernando, higher up on the same stream, and at Achaguas to the south. By 25th May, 1819, Bolívar was in the neighbourhood of Achaguas, and held a review of his troops at Mantecal, on one of the tributaries of the Apure south-west of San Fernando. He had 1,300 infantry and 700 cavalry, including his International Brigades of English, Scots, Irish, French, Germans, Poles and Italians. They brought a knowledge of modern warfare gained in the Napoleonic campaigns, combined with the ideas and ideals of revolutionary Europe. From the first Bolívar saw that their value would be ideological as well as military, and he mixed the International Brigaders with his own men, so that the new ideas spread rapidly among his Venezuelan troops. But there were enough volunteers from Britain to form a whole battalion, and this was always treated as a separate unit.

Bolívar's plan involved moving a force of 2,000 men through a country which had practically no provisions except cattle "on the hoof"; no roads, no bridges, swollen rivers and swampy plains. A Venezuelan novelist, Rómulo Gallegos, has described what travelling in that country is like, even in the dry season. "On he went fording the tributaries of the Guárico, with water up to the saddle; putting up noisy flights of duck and heron, and lulled to a doze by the ceaseless *clop-clop* of his horse in the muddy pools. On he rode towards the upper Apure, along the green immensity of the broad banks. He started with his shadow in front, stretching long on the trail before him; he passed over it, and then had it at his back, long on the trail once more. But he was always in the middle of the plain, the centre of a circle of mirages, where the savannah melted away, calcined by the sun before it became converted into sky. He passed dense palm-groves, and green reed-beds where the clear water reflected the gold of dawn and the purple of twilight. Then he crossed the desolate tablelands, wastes of withered grass, which the sun burnt and consumed. A melancholy cry, as of the driver of imaginary herds, turned to a song; and the song became a cry again, that spread out and died away in the breadth of the silence. So he went on, trying to forget his loneliness, numbed by a prospect which was always the same, but always held something new."

Conditions of service were hard. The volunteers from Europe had to put up with the pestilential climate of the plains of the Orinoco, the unknown and dreaded tropical diseases, and the shortage or entire absence of nearly everything they needed. Their rations were two pieces of jerked beef (*tasajo*) and casaba flour (*cazabe*); they drank water from the rivers and streams. Their quarters were a primitive hut, a hammock (*chinchorro*) or a hide mat which was often harder to lie on than the bare, wet ground. Their uniforms soon fell to pieces from exposure to sun and rain, and they dressed like the native *llaneros* : shorts, a plaid (*cobija*), a wide straw hat, bare legs and often bare feet. They were nearly all young: Bolívar himself was 36; Soublette, chief of staff, 29; Santander, commanding the leading division, 28; Anzoátegui, with the rear-guard, 30.

Bolívar's plan was to keep the Royalists occupied with his *llanero* cavalry outside San Fernando, Barinas and Cúcuta, while the infantry marched along the right bank of the Apure to Guasdalito, and then into the territory of New Granada, by crossing the Arauca into the fearful swamps of the province of Casanare. He was joined on 11th June, 1819, by Santander with another 1,200 men. They decided to approach the high Colombian plateau by way of the Páramo de Pisba, a cold upland, not likely to be well guarded by the Spaniards. On 22nd June, the combined Colombian and Venezuelan forces, now numbering 2,275 men, began to climb up to the Páramo through Pore and Paya. Three weeks' marching brought them into the Andes, where their first engagement (Paya, 27th June) was a success: the Spanish advance guard of 300 men was dislodged from a position "so strong by nature," Bolívar reported, "that 100 men might have held it against 1,000."

Having dispersed the troops opposed to them,

the liberators began to ascend to the Páramo. The trail led through thick woods of dripping trees. In places the path was "simply a steep, narrow stairway of moss-covered rocks," with a stream at the bottom and jagged stones projecting from its dripping sides. Sometimes it was so steep and slippery that the loads had to be taken off the pack-animals and carried up by hand. Between 9,000 and 10,000 feet the forest ceased, and they came to the edge of the Páramo; "the cold, damp wilderness that occupies the summit of the Cordillera, a bleak area of damp, chilly fogs, solitary ponds, and a scrubby growth of dwarfed, thorny plants." It was difficult to realize that the unimpressive hills which rose above the general level of the plateau were in reality the peaks of the Andes, 12,000 and 14,000 feet above the sea. The cold was intense, damp and penetrating.

For four days (2nd to 6th July) they scrambled over the slippery paths and treacherous bogs of this melancholy, inhospitable, mountain wilderness. There was no view; the bitter wind blew the clouds all about them. The few *llaneros* who had remained, and "the impassive English," who declared that they would follow Bolívar anywhere—to Cape Horn, if he wished it—went grimly forward in the cold rain and the biting wind. Bolívar, wrapped in a great scarlet cloak, was indomitable; but even the devoted aide-de-camp, O'Leary, almost gave up. Many died of exposure, including 56 of the English, and when the rest reached Socha (6th July, 1819) they had practically nothing on but their weapons. All the pack and saddle animals had died on the way. The sick and stragglers were brought in, together with the arms of those who had died on the march; but the liberating troops were made much of by the inhabitants and provided with such comforts and pack-animals as were to be had.

Bolívar and his men were not long in recovering from the effects of their march across the Andes. They moved south from Socha, through Tasco and Corrales towards the River Sogamoso. The treeless wastes had been left behind, and they were now in a pleasant land of lazy streams and long lines of poplars. Between 10th and 15th July they had three engagements. At Pantano de Vargas on the 25th, Barreiro, the Spanish commander was in a strong position, while that of the liberators was described as "extraordinarily unfavourable." The Spanish troops included battalions of crack regiments: Numancia and the King's Own. They were attacked by a column headed by some companies of the British Legion, who charged with such intrepidity that the Spaniards were dislodged, though they rallied and both sides lost heavily. The result seemed a drawn battle. Actually it was the decisive action of the campaign. The battle ended in a heavy downpour, and after dark Barreiro withdrew to Paipa. Bolívar also returned to his encampment, but he was now free to get in between the Spaniards and Bogotá. On 6th August he received information that they were about to move back to join forces with the Viceroy; and next morning he climbed a hill with a spy-glass to see which road they would take. As soon as he saw them pass the point at which the road forked, and realized that they would go by Boyacá, he ordered his force to proceed to the bridge as quickly as possible. The Spaniards got there first; but they were surprised soon after their mid-day meal to see Bolívar's men suddenly emerging from the ferns and foliage on the banks of the stream. The *llanero* cavalry found a ford lower down, and attacked them in the rear; while the British went at the Spanish in front. General Santander, who commanded the left, and who had at first met with "temerarious resistance," completed the operation. The Spanish army, hemmed in on every side, eventually laid down its arms and surrendered, with the commander, General Barreiro, the second-in-command, and many other officers. When the news reached Santa Fe de Bogotá, the Viceroy hurriedly departed. "The precipitation" (Soublette wrote in his official report) "with which the Viceroy and his satellites fled on the first news of the issue of the battle of Boyacá, prevented his saving anything of the public treasure. In the mint we have found about half a million dollars, in metal; and in the other public buildings, all the material of war to equip a numerous army. The liberty of New Granada has infallibly established that of all South America, and the year 1819 will see the end of the war which Spain has waged against us, with such violations of humanity, since the year 1810."

Bolívar rode into Santa Fe the next afternoon (10th August, 1819) almost alone. "The liberating army," the dispatch reported, "has performed what it undertook in this campaign. In 75 days' march from the village of Mantecal, in the province of Barinas, his Excellency has made his entry into the capital of the New Kingdom [of Granada], after having overcome difficulties and obstacles much greater than could be foreseen when this expedition was undertaken, and destroyed an army three times superior in number to the invaders."

While these events had been taking place in New Granada, Páez was keeping the Royalists fully occupied in the interior of Venezuela. Bolívar, profiting by his past experience, determined to prosecute the war with the utmost vigour, sending out his commanders after the retreating Royalists; but by December he was back in Angostura, where certain high officers and members of the Congress had been intriguing against him under the supposition that the march across the Andes into New Granada was bound to fail. Bolívar could afford to be magnanimous; intrigues and intriguers were forgotten. His entry into Angostura was "one of the most gratifying and affecting spectacles since the days of Washington." He was hailed by the whole population as the liberator and father of his country, the destroyer of oppression and victor over tyranny; and now at last one of his great ambitions was about to be achieved. On 17th December, 1819, the "fundamental law of the Republic of Colombia" was published, and subsequently approved by Congress, by which the old Captaincy-General of Venezuela and the Viceroyalty of the New Kingdom of Granada were united in one single state, under the title of the Republic of Colombia. It was divided into three departments: Venezuela, Quito (the modern Ecuador) and Cundinamarca (the modern Colombia); the capitals of these departments were the cities of Caracas, Quito and Bogotá, which henceforth was to drop the addition of Santa Fe. The debts of the republics, which had been contracted for carrying on the war, were acknowledged and funded into one. This "fundamental law" was, of course, premature. A large part of the country was still in the hands of the Spanish Royalists; but Bolívar was confident of his power to liberate not only that, but the greater part of South America also, from the dominion of Spain. The law was barely passed, when the Liberator set out once more (on 24th December, 1819) on the ten weeks' ride back to New Granada.

By 1820 it seemed possible that independence might be obtained without further fighting. In Spain, the liberal movement associated with the name of Colonel Riego and the inspiriting tune of his famous "Hymn"—the Republican National Anthem—forced Ferdinand to return to the Constitution of 1812, and instructions were sent to the Spanish authorities in South America to effect a reconciliation with the Republican leaders. The part played by Spaniards themselves in the liberation of their American colonies was described not long ago by a correspondent of *The Times Literary Supplement* (26th Feb., 1944). The Spanish army of reconquest assembled at Cadiz was liberal in sentiment; officers and men disliked the idea of imposing by force on the Spanish American colonies a system of absolutism which they heartily detested at home, and all sorts of pretexts were employed so as not to be embarked on a mission which they considered to be as hopeless as it was tyrannical. They were not alone, in Spain. Behind them were the powerful "Secret Societies" (i.e. freemasons) led by men of distinction such as Alcalá Galiano and Mendizábal who later took refuge in England, when in 1823 Ferdinand went back on his word and ordered Riego to be hanged. In 1820, however, Ferdinand was afraid; and he published a proclamation to his South American subjects—a curious and pathetic document, a last effort by Imperial Spain to recover its lost authority by vain promises and empty threats. It was believed in Madrid that the inhabitants of Colombia would submit themselves to the same constitution as the people of the Peninsula—to that Cortes by which the atrocities of Monteverde and the other irregular Royalist leaders had, in ignorance, been condoned and encouraged. The Constitution of Cadiz was duly proclaimed; but it was no longer enough. The time had gone by when more of the inhabitants of Colombia were for the King than for the Republic. The *mestizos*, the "browns," and even the *llaneros*, the cowboys of the great plains, were now all for independence.

An eye-witness relates that when Morillo, the Royalist commander, received the instructions from his government, he remarked: "They are mad. They do not know what they are doing. They do not know the country or the enemy, the actions or the conditions. Yet they want me to go through the humiliation of negotiating with these people! I will do it, because it is my duty: subordination and obedience." He wrote to Bolívar and the other Republican leaders, informing them that he had given orders to his divisional commanders to suspend hostilities for a month. He then found that he had to submit to further humiliation: the terms did not go nearly far enough. The Republicans were no longer content with a return to the Constitution of Cadiz and subordination to the government at home. He did not break off negotiations, however, and eventually nominated plenipotentiaries to discuss terms. Bolívar included two of his most trusted supporters: Sucre and Briceño Méndez; and on the 25th November, 1820, they signed an armistice with the Spanish Royalists. The Republicans were no longer "insurgents"; they had won the right to be treated as equals, a recognition of the fact that since the declaration of Venezuelan independence in 1811, the war had been no longer a civil war but an international one. The armistice was to continue for six months, during which time commissioners would be sent to Spain to discuss a reconciliation. The Republicans had been clever in the negotiations; they stood to gain either recognition of their independence from the Spanish Government, or time to reorganize their forces for final victory. Morillo and Bolívar met on the most friendly terms, on 27th November, at the tiny village of Santa Ana—a scene vividly described by O'Leary, who was present. The two commanders dined together, and eventually slept in the same room. Morillo wrote home an account in which O'Leary's is confirmed.

> "I have just come back from the village of Santa Ana, where yesterday I spent one of the pleasantest days of my life in the company of Bolívar and various members of his staff. Bolívar came alone with them, in complete good faith and friendliness, and I immediately sent away the small escort I had with me.

You cannot imagine how interesting the interview was, or the cordiality which reigned at it. We were all wildly happy; and it seemed like a dream to be meeting there like Spaniards, brothers and friends. You can believe me that we were frank and open with one another! Bolívar was wildly excited; we embraced again and again, and determined to put up a monument to the perpetual memory of our meeting, on the spot at which we embraced for the first time."

Morillo returned to Spain to convince the government of the necessity of speedily concluding a peace with the Colombians. His admiration for Bolívar was genuine; and it was still vivid many years afterwards, when two of Bolívar's most devoted friends, O'Leary and Soublette, visited Morillo at Corunna, and were given many letters and documents concerning the Liberator's life.

Bolívar sent two representatives to Spain to negotiate peace on the basis of recognition of Colombian independence, i.e. that of Venezuela, New Granada and Quito. On other points he was willing to compromise; he was prepared to offer Panamá in exchange for that part of the former Presidency of Quito still in Spanish occupation; he would accept an alliance with Spain, offensive or defensive, but not a king—neither a Bourbon nor a member of any other reigning house in Europe. It was useless. The Spanish Government did not understand the situation as well as Morillo did. In Spain the revolutions in South America were still regarded as mere insurrections; the claim to independence was held to be inadmissible, and the two Colombian representatives were not recognized in Madrid or given any official status.

When Bolívar was informed that all efforts for peace would break down before the intransigeance of Ferdinand and his ministers, he decided to renew hostilities. Colombia had not been entirely peaceful. In January 1821 the Ecuadorian province of Cuenca had already seceded from the Colombian Union, and several other districts had followed their lead. Bolívar was unaware of these manœuvres, but he had had time to reorganize his forces, while the Royalists had received no reinforcements worth mention from Spain; and it had been possible for him to remove Venezuelan troops from unhealthy districts during the rainy season. Strategically, too, the Republicans now had the advantage; the Royalists only held Cumaná and part of the province of Caracas. Again, desertions were taking place from the Royalists to the Republicans. Reyes Vargas, an Indian descended from the ancient Caciques, who was a colonel in the Spanish service, notified his defection from the Royalist cause in an energetic proclamation. "Born a Colombian, I am once more a Colombian. . . . The convulsions of our ancient mother country have given me important lessons on the rights of men: Spain herself has taught me that even a king is but the subject of his people, . . . [and] I have become convinced that the Spanish and the American peoples equally possess the right of establishing a government consistent with their own opinions, and for their own prosperity."

On 10th March, 1821, Bolívar addressed a letter to La Torre, Spanish commander-in-chief after the departure of Morillo, in which he alleged that the scarcity of provisions under which the army of the Apure laboured would compel him to renew hostilities unless the Spanish Government acceded to his just and reasonable demands. To this, La Torre replied, that in conformity with the twelfth article of the armistice, military operations would begin again after forty days. This period had hardly gone by when one of the Republican commanders advanced on the capital. He had been too precipitate, and was easily repulsed; the first round there, and at La Guaira, went to the Royalists.

Bolívar by this time had a trained force of 6,500 men, together with a British battalion and 1,500 *llanero* cavalry. He had always wanted to try another engagement on the plain of Carabobo and on 24th June, 1821, the opportunity presented itself. The plain of Carabobo lies 2,000 feet above the sea, commanding the approaches from the south to both Valencia and Caracas. There are not many trees; but the slopes are covered with tall grass or dense scrub. It is difficult to move, except by the regular trails, and the approaches to these had been covered by the Spanish commander. Bolívar was observing the Spanish position from the hill of Buenavista, five miles off. He saw about 5,000 men posted on the edge of the plain in such a way as to make a frontal attack too costly to be worth while. The Spanish gun-positions, in particular, seemed to command the only way by which an approach might be made from the south or east. Then he was told of a little-known trail which came out on to the plain from the west; and he sent Páez with his rough-riding *llaneros* and the British battalion to take the Royalists on the flank. The path was so narrow that the men had to march in single file. Sometimes they were in the bed of a swiftly running stream, sometimes on a steep hillside, sometimes making their way through tropical scrub under a hot sun. After two hours and a half, they suddenly came out on the crest of a hill, in full view of the Spanish force nearly two miles away on the plain below. Páez and his rough-riders went charging down the hill; but they had misjudged the distance and also the ground before them, and were caught in a ravine they had not noticed, about 150 feet below the level of the plain. The Spaniards had seen them, and brought up guns and men; the patriots seemed caught in a trap, for the *llaneros* could not stand the concentrated fire of veteran infantry and artillery. Here, however, the British came in. They formed a hollow square, and though they lost 600 out of 900, they held steady until the *llaneros* could re-form and climb the slope again, rather more to the Spanish rear. That was the moment when Bolívar attacked in front; and when the *llanero* lancers got on to the plain and took the Royalists in the rear, nothing could stand against them. In little more than an hour it was all over: whole companies of Spanish infantry were destroyed or rounded up as prisoners; very few got back to Valencia.

The second battle of Carabobo was one of the decisive battles of the war. The Spanish commander shut himself up with the remnant of his forces in Puerto Cabello, which was to be the last refuge of Spanish domination in Venezuela. Bolívar moved at once on Caracas, where the garrison capitulated; officers and men were allowed to embark at La Guaira, on condition that they took no further part in the war, while others joined the Republican army. The days of *guerra a muerte* were over, and independence was in sight.

Chapter Seven

Bolívar and San Martín

"GREAT COLOMBIA," or the Colombian Union, was free—that is to say, the modern states of Colombia and Venezuela were now independent of Spain. The reason which made the renewal of war necessary was the refusal of the Spanish Government to accept the fact of Colombian independence. To Bolívar, that was fundamental; he refused to negotiate on any other terms. Spain must recognize the new Republic. But since recognition was not forthcoming, the only way of making independence certain was to attack the Spanish forces in the south; and Bolívar had already made plans for carrying the war to Quito and Peru.

The Presidency of Quito—a territory considerably more extensive than the modern Republic of Ecuador which has inherited it—had originally formed part of "The New Kingdom of Granada." An attempt at independence, in 1809, had been ruthlessly suppressed; the port of Guayaquil alone had succeeded, in 1820, in deposing the Royalist authorities and forming an independent administration under Joaquín de Olmedo, afterwards well known as a poet and man of letters. In 1822 the port was under the protection of Colombia; and when Quito was captured for Bolívar by a liberating force under General Sucre, Guayaquil, with the rest of the modern territory of Ecuador, was included, with Venezuela, in "Great Colombia."

A congress, which met at Cúcuta, had elected Bolívar President of the Colombian Union and Santander Vice-President. Bolívar accepted unwillingly. He only wanted to get on with the war: to drive the Royalists out of Peru so that there should be no threat to Colombia from the south; and the terms of his message to congress were a genuine expression of his military and political anxieties.

"Since our public calamities drove me to take up arms for the liberation of my country," he began, "I have kept up the struggle for eleven years—not with the idea of gaining control of the government for myself, but in the firm resolve never to exercise it. I vowed that I would never be more than a soldier; that I would only serve in war, and in peace become once more an ordinary citizen. I am not the kind of ruler the Republic wants. A soldier, first by necessity and perhaps now by inclination, my destiny lies in camp or in barracks. For me, an office-desk is a place of punishment; all my natural instincts are against it. And if, after what I have said, Congress should persist in confiding to me the executive power of the State, I will only yield through obedience, admitting the title of

President for the duration of the war on condition that I am authorized to continue the campaign at the head of the army, leaving the government of the country in the hands of General Santander, who has so justly deserved his election by this house as Vice-President of the Republic."

Bolívar's conditions were accepted; and during his long absence in Peru the affairs of Great Colombia were in the hands of two men who, in spite of wide differences in education and character, were agreed on one thing: to betray Bolívar and dissolve the union between Colombia and Venezuela. Vice-President Santander was a cultured man and an administrator, less a soldier than a politician, who supported Bolívar in the campaigns in Ecuador and Peru, but bided his time to become leader of the opposition and turn Bolívar out. Páez, leader of the *llanero* rough-riders, was against all lawyers and politicians; but he had a shrewd understanding and was ready to be led, even by the politicians, if they could flatter his ambition to become leader of the separatists. Bolívar himself had no illusions on the character or ambitions of his subordinates. He invariably wrote friendly letters to both of them; but he saw through the motives of Santander, and summed up the character of Páez in a few words:

"You can have no idea," he wrote to Dr. Gual, "of the way the minds of some of our leaders work. They are not the kind of man you know. They are a kind you do *not* know: men who have been fighting for a long time and think themselves highly deserving, but feel humiliated and miserable because they have no hope of keeping all that they have won in the war. They are determined *llaneros* who have never regarded themselves on a level with other men who know more and seem better than they are. Even I, who have had them under my command, still do not know what they are capable of and treat them with the greatest respect; but that is not enough to inspire them with that frankness and confidence which ought to exist between comrades and fellow-citizens. Believe me, Gual, we are on the edge of an abyss, or rather on the top of a volcano ready for eruption. I fear peace more than war."

Bolívar was a good judge of the character of his subordinates. He saw through Páez, though he promoted him on the field of Carabobo; but that did not prevent the *llanero* leader from becoming in a few years the greatest enemy of united Colombia. The most trustworthy of the younger commanders, Antonio José de Sucre, Bolívar took with him to the south.

"Sucre is the best-organized brain in Colombia," he said afterwards. "He is methodical, yet capable of the highest flights of imagination. He is the best general in the Republic, and the first statesman. He knows how to persuade men, as well as lead them."

Only troops with that personal devotion which Bolívar was able to inspire would have followed him now. It was a prospect even more forbidding than his march from Angostura to Bogotá and his crossing of the Andes. Some of the men had marched from Valencia, near the north coast of Venezuela to Popayán, in the south of Colombia, over a thousand miles through country where there were next to no roads, flooded plains, burning deserts and bitter mountain winds. But they were ready to follow Bolívar anywhere because he made the army his first consideration; the unreliable recruits of his first years had become the invincible battalions of disciplined men who knew what they were fighting for.

At the beginning of March, 1822, Bolívar started from Popayán, a charming town 5,700 feet above sea-level in the heart of the Colombian Andes. His route lay southwards, through the grim and hostile Pasto country, a plateau, lying at 8,000 feet, in the extreme south-east of the country. The population, which was largely Indian, was aggressively Royalist and clerical, and the march seemed afterwards to Bolívar one of the most unpleasant he had ever made. They entered the Presidency of Quito by Ipiales and Tulcán, nearly 10,000 feet above the Pacific; and the whole campaign was conducted at this extreme altitude, with a background of some of the highest mountains in the world: Cotopaxi

(19,643 ft.), and Chimborazo (20,494 ft.). Bolívar did not have things all his own way, but he won the battle of Bomboná on the 7th April, 1822, and Sucre was successful at Rio Bamba on the 22nd April and at Pichincha on the 24th May. The former Presidency of Quito was incorporated into Great Colombia.

There is little doubt that Bolívar, personally, would have liked to leave things as they were at this stage, and go home. He would return first to Bogotá, resign the presidency—the whole of the Republic of Colombia was now free of Spanish Royalists—and then go back to Caracas for a long rest with his family. A letter of 21st June, 1822, to his old friends, the Marqués del Toro and his brother Fernando, shows that this plan was in his mind. But the project came to nothing. On 11th July he was called to Guayaquil, where a grave question was under discussion: should the port be an independent state, or part of Colombia, or belong to Peru? Through Bolívar's efforts, the second solution was adopted, the only reasonable one; Guayaquil was geographically and economically the port of the provinces of Quito, which had now become part of the Colombian Union and had no connexion with Peru except that some wealthy Peruvians owned property there.

Then, suddenly and unexpectedly on 25th July, 1822, he received a visit from the Argentine general José de San Martín.

San Martín was the greatest Argentine of his time, and the best soldier in South America. The inhabitants of Buenos Aires and the River Plate provinces had been lucky in their escape from Spanish rule. After years of neglect from their mother country they had been visited by a filibustering expedition from the Cape of Good Hope. British troops landed and occupied Buenos Aires in 1806. When the inhabitants had recovered from their surprise, they found it comparatively easy to get rid of the invaders; and another expedition, rashly sent out from England in the following year, failed through the dilatory methods of the commander, General Whitelocke.

The idea of the invasion and occupation of the River Plate was never taken very seriously by the British Government; but it was an idea that was by no means new. As early as 1703 suggestions for the capture and colonization by England and the Dutch of the Spanish possessions in South America had been made in an anonymous pamphlet entitled *Europa libera*. Again in 1711 a proposal was made by "a person of distinction," "to send in the next October eight Men of War with five or six large Transports, which number of ships may very well contain 2,500 men fit to land upon any occasion, to attack or rather seize upon Buenos Ayres, which is situated upon the River of Plate." The author believed that a British colony there would secure great trade advantages to Britain, and his anonymous pamphlet on the subject was published about 1727.

The invasions of 1806 and 1807 taught the people of Buenos Aires that they could manage their own affairs with no help from home. The Spanish Viceroy had been of no use, and they appointed one of their own—Jacques Liniers, a Frenchman—and freed themselves through their own efforts. Then they had been fortunate when the Spanish Government had decided to send Morillo and his expedition to Venezuela, and not to the River Plate. Venezuela had suffered, and suffered horribly, under the full weight of the Spanish attempt at reconquest; and the "United Provinces of the River Plate" looked like becoming the most important political group in South America, until Bolívar seemed to challenge them with his hardly won and precariously united "Great Colombia."

Argentine statesmen had realized, as Bolívar had, that independence would never be secure so long as the Spaniards held Peru. That also was realized by San Martín.

San Martín was not an irregular popular leader —a *caudillo*; he was very much the professional soldier. He lived "rough" and talked "rough," like the troops; and his simple, barrack-room manners have given him a halo of romantic, democratic popularity—like that of Artigas, the sympathetic, Garibaldian hero of Uruguay—a form of popularity denied to the Liberator.

Bolívar could live level with a *llanero* or a marquess; but he swore like an officer and a gentleman, while San Martín was a soldier first and last and swore like a sergeant. Born in the remote riverside village of Yapeyú, formerly a mission-settlement, on the west or Argentine bank of the River Uruguay, he had been educated in Spain for a military career, and served in the Spanish army. In the Peninsular War he met Lord Macduff (afterwards Earl of Fife), who saw his uncommon military genius and became a firm friend. It was through him that San Martín was able to get out of Spain, when he decided to take "French leave" from the Spanish army and offer his services to the new government of the River Plate.

He sailed from London in January 1812. Some of his fellow-passengers had been members of a masonic lodge at Cadiz: and San Martín resolved to found something of the same kind in Buenos Aires. He had seen how valuable it could be, for patriotic purposes, in the group which gathered in London at the house in Grafton Street where Miranda had once lived, and which was afterwards occupied by Andrés Bello. San Martín was not exactly the man for fantastic notions and queer ritual; but the discipline and silence of the group impressed him, as did its mathematical and military symbolism, and he resolved to make use of them in America. Promoted Colonel and given command of a regiment of mounted grenadiers, he found himself posted with two of his travelling companions who had sailed in the same ship from London. They formed a "triangle" and a "workshop," and the movement soon spread its cells through the provinces of the River Plate. They took the name of *Lautaro* for their "lodge," Lautaro being a character in *La Araucana*, Ercilla's epic poem on the conquest of Chile, the Indian who proclaims the liberty of his country from the Spaniards and begins the struggle for independence.

Doubt has been thrown on the masonic character of the Lautaro Lodge; but the masonic symbolism is evident, even if the lodge was not strictly a masonic foundation. There were already masonic establishments in Buenos Aires, dating back to 1795; and in 1806, and after the British invasions, there were three lodges of British origin, which certainly helped to spread the idea of independence from Spain. It is worth remembering that Miranda and Bolívar were both masons—though the latter took it no more seriously than Pierre in *War and Peace*. So too were Washington, Franklin, Adams, Hamilton and Lafayette; San Martín's Scottish friend, Macduff; Popham, Cochrane, and other Englishmen concerned with the emancipation of Spanish America. The political implications of freemasonry as a force against oppression and bigotry had been illustrated in various ways during the eighteenth century; the most striking instance, perhaps, is

Mozart's masonic opera, *The Magic Flute.* The sense of initiation, universal brotherhood and liberal idealism would have appealed strongly to a man of the noble simplicity of character of San Martín. The Lautaro Lodge, whether it was masonic or not, kept up the discipline and mystery of the "craft," and made use of masonic symbols to such an extent that in 1816, Pueyrredón, at that time head of the government of Buenos Aires, requested San Martín not to employ those symbols in official correspondence, though there is no document actually proving that San Martín was a mason himself.

Not long after his return to South America, San Martín was ordered (in 1814) to form and train an army in the Andes, to cope with the Spanish menace in Chile and Peru. The first Chilean independents had been crushed at Rancagua; but some of the survivors made their way across the Andes to Mendoza, where San Martín received them with open arms. He was a thorough soldier, and took few chances. Without haste he trained and equipped his Argentine and Chilean forces by the best European methods; but he refused to move across the Andes until he had everything he wanted and until he was quite ready. He was perpetually applying to the government in Buenos Aires for such articles as muskets, sabres, jerked beef, tents, shirts and *ponchos*: blankets with a hole in the middle, so that they can also be used as capes. He was particularly insistent on the necessity for bugles; without bugles the army could not march. Pueyrredón ransacked the country for these things, and after hunting all over Buenos Aires sent him the only two bugles in the place, carefully packed in a small wooden box. San Martín, he complained, seemed to want the world, the flesh and the devil. But he got them; government officials who were obstructive, or said that it could not be done, were removed from their posts or given appointments elsewhere, and *el mundo*, *el demonio* and *la carne* were duly loaded on pack-animals and sent from Buenos Aires to the foot of the Andes, a distance of between 600 and 700 miles.

Then, in January 1817, San Martín, having craftily misled the Spaniards as to which trail he proposed to take, led his men across the Andes on a march which rivals Bolívar's in courage and endurance, though it was unlike Bolívar's in leaving nothing to chance. San Martín had more and better material than Bolívar had; he had not to march up to the mountains from water-logged, tropical plains; his crossing was made 1,000 feet lower than Bolívar's (at 12,000 ft. compared with 13,000 ft.), and he did not lose nearly so many men. But like Bolívar he had to pass through a bare country with no roads; there was no game or pasture of any sort, and he lost a third of his horses and nearly half of his mules, while the rest arrived on the Chilean side of the Andes in a condition that was deplorable. Most of his men suffered from mountain sickness, and many died from the intense cold. Still, it was a numerous and well-trained Argentine force that crossed the Andes into Chile; and when they joined the Chilean patriots under O'Higgins, they won decisive battles at Chacabuco (12th February, 1817) and Maipó (5th April, 1818) which effectively put an end to Spanish dominion in Chile. The Army of the Andes then embarked (August 1820) in Lord Cochrane's ships, and was carried northward to Peru.

Peru was the last and greatest stronghold of Spanish power in America. Its wealth and the natural easy-going ways of the inhabitants, produced by the enervating climate of the coastal regions—and more particularly in Lima the capital—had discouraged movements of independence. Some progress was made, however, after the arrival of San Martín in September 1820, and he had assumed the title of "Protector of Peru." In matters of local government he was certainly well-advised. In Chile, the new administration was built up within the framework of the ancient assembly convoked by the *cabildo* of Santiago; and in Peru, too, the success of the whole plan depended on the adherence of the inhabitants and the favourable votes of the *cabildos*. Bolívar had done much the same.

The Protector was undoubtedly an excellent soldier, a commander admired and respected by his own men. Though he had not the magical personality of Bolívar, he made a very good impression on British naval men and other British representatives who saw him; but his political ideas seemed to Bolívar, and to many of his contemporaries in Colombia and Venezuela, curiously "un-American." San Martín, like some others in Buenos Aires, was in favour of monarchy —not for himself, like Itúrbide in Mexico—but for a member of one of the ruling families in Europe. Monarchy seemed likely to make the Portuguese dominion of Brazil great and powerful; why should it not do the same for the Spanish-speaking American countries? San Martín's plan gradually took the form of a reconciliation between Peru and Spain on a basis of the restoration of the monarchy; and on 7th June, 1821, in negotiations at a place called Punchauca, he offered to come to terms with the Spanish Viceroy. Independence was to be accepted by the Spaniards, with a regency under the Viceroy, who would govern independently until the arrival of a prince of the royal family of Spain. In the end, the Viceroy declined; the Spanish Government could not agree to independence. Negotiations were dropped. But on 6th July, 1821, the Viceroy, considering his position unsafe, evacuated Lima, unmolested by San Martín's troops, and San Martín was invited to enter the city. On 28th July, 1821, he proclaimed the viceroyalty of Peru at an end and the country independent of Spain.

The restoration of monarchy in Spanish-speaking America and the establishment of Spanish princes there as late as 1821 would probably have proved more difficult than San Martín imagined. One thing essential to monarchy is a continuous tradition, and that was only possible in the schemes which had already been proposed by two European statesmen: the Elder Pitt, for North America, and Aranda, for Mexico and the southern half of the continent. Aranda's part in the scheme has been questioned; but it was revived afterwards—when the time for it had already gone by—by Godoy, the "Prince of Peace." In these projects, members of the British and Spanish royal families were to be sent out to the colonies like governors-general and then raised to the status of independent princes, while the King at home would take the title of emperor. In the second half of the eighteenth century when these schemes were proposed monarchy might have been established in America without any period of transition, as it was achieved later—though for different reasons—when the Portuguese royal family emigrated to Brazil, and Brazil and not Portugal became the seat of an emperor. But now, after ten years of war, the Spanish-speaking countries in America had set up governments of their own. All sense of continuity with the Spanish monarchy, or of dependence on the Spanish Crown, had been broken. Republican ideals had widened the breach between Spain and America, and made reconciliation difficult if not impossible. Finally, there was the question of national psychology. It would have been difficult for any Spanish government to be reconciled with former Spanish colonies after recognizing their independence. It took the British Government a good many years—and a war—to be reconciled with the United States. Even the Spanish liberals refused to countenance the autonomy of the overseas dominions, and the Cortes of Cadiz (whose liberalism seemed, to many British statesmen, excessive) only gave grudging and very limited consent to the reforms proposed by the deputies who represented the Spanish colonies.

Bolívar's ideas were very different. He had already pointed out, when negotiating the armistice in Venezuela, that a prince of the House of Bourbon could not be accepted as ruler of Colombia in any circumstances. But San Martín, when his schooner was signalled coming up the estuary to Guayaquil on 25th July, 1822, seems to have thought that Bolívar would support his monarchist plans for the future of Peru, as well as his designs for securing for Peru the port of Guayaquil itself.

San Martín's visit was unexpected. Bolívar hastened to send his senior aide-de-camp with a letter regretting that he had no time to prepare a public welcome worthy of the Protector of Peru. The letter was accompanied by a more personal one, expressed in the friendliest terms.

There was a great public reception: the streets were lined with troops, and a salute of 21 guns was fired from each of the three forts. The two leaders met twice the next day, and had a long interview on the following afternoon, probably in the thatched, one-storey house still preserved and pointed out as the place of the historic meeting. There were four questions which San Martín wished to discuss: (1) the future of Guayaquil; (2) the replacement of the losses suffered by the Argentine and Chilean contingents which had fought in the campaign for Quito; (3) the amount of armed support to be contributed by Colombia to the liberation of Peru; and (4) an agreement for the establishment of monarchical government in that part of South America.

A great deal has been published about the celebrated interview at Guayaquil. Nationalist feelings and wishful thinking have tended to obscure the truth—or the historical evidence for the truth—for the conferences were held behind closed doors, and at the first meeting even the private secretaries were excluded, though they were in attendance in the next room. The most authentic document is the report made by Bolívar's first secretary, Colonel José Gabriel Pérez, on the day after the meeting, and forwarded to the Colombian Government at Bogotá. It was not discovered until long afterwards (in 1906) and is the only official account of what was discussed at the meetings, though it naturally takes Bolívar's point of view. Next in importance is a private letter from Bolívar to Vice-President Santander, written on the day after San Martín left; and both this and the secretary's report confirm the statement made long afterwards by Mosquera, another of Bolívar's secretaries who was present. There is nothing from San Martín comparable in importance to these, until we come to the letters written some weeks later to O'Higgins; and the reports of what he said to his staff on the voyage back, and, long afterwards, to the English General Miller.

According to the report of Bolívar's first secretary, the Protector remarked that he had nothing more to say on the affairs of Guayaquil, in which he had no right to interfere. What had been done was the fault of the people of Guayaquil themselves. Bolívar replied that he thought San Martín's fears would be allayed by consulting the inhabitants. On the 28th of the month the assembly would meet, and he counted on a majority of votes for the incorporation of Guayaquil in Colombia.

The question of Guayaquil, then, gave no ground for discussion; it was already settled. The port had been legally incorporated in Colombia along with Quito, and the territories of the former Presidency, in accordance with the legal principle by which the former Spanish territories, on attaining their independence, kept the boundaries which they had had in 1810. The claim that

Guayaquil belonged to Peru had no legal standing, while the claim that it should be independent had no common sense. San Martín disliked lawyers almost as much as did Páez; but he had to accept the logic of the situation.

The question of the losses to Argentine and Chilean troops, and the sending of Colombian troops to Peru, depended on the fact that the independent Peruvian Government in Lima was still threatened by several formations of Spanish regular troops, which San Martín had allowed to retire undisturbed to the high, healthy uplands, after they had evacuated Lima and let him in. Lima was always something of a Capua, and had a fatal and demoralizing effect on whichever army occupied it. To make certain of the independence of Peru, it was necessary to have the assistance of Bolívar's trained and victorious Colombians and Venezuelans, 1,800 of whom were sent, with 600 more to replace casualties among the Argentine and Chilean troops under San Martín. The question of sending troops of the Colombian Union led inevitably to the type of government most suitable to Peru after victory had been won. The Colombian army was stoutly republican, and unlikely to fight under a commander who was willing to accept a return to monarchy.

The question of monarchy or republic was the chief reason why the two leaders could not agree. It was not a question of how many Colombian troops should be sent; nor yet—as San Martín believed—a question of who should command them. There seems to be no justification for the statement that Bolívar would not trust his troops to San Martín, or would not accept San Martín's generous offer to serve under him. San Martín also misunderstood the constitutional position of Bolívar: as president of the Colombian Republic as well as commander of its armed forces, Bolívar could not possibly take his troops into Peru without being authorized to do so by his own government, the Colombian Congress. San Martín's position was different. He was in command of a mixed force of Argentines and Chileans; he had had no contact with the government in Buenos Aires for many months, and had, indeed, been practically disowned by them.

The difference of opinion between the Liberator and the Protector was not due to personal jealousy or ambition. Their disagreement was not over the means of achieving independence from Spain, but over the political solution to be adopted when independence had been gained. San Martín wanted princes from Europe; Bolívar, "without rejecting the idea outright, was for founding republics with presidents holding office for life, with the powers, prerogatives and limitations of a King of England, but in any case of South American birth, and governing through parliaments elected on popular suffrage."

It gradually appeared that agreement was

impossible. Bolívar could not feel sure that San Martín was not committed in advance to some monarchist project. His information service was too good for him not to have heard of the negotiations at Punchauca; in fact his correspondence shows that he was aware of them; but it did not occur to him that San Martín might have been merely improvising his policy in so guileless a fashion and with a lack of foresight which he would never have allowed in preparing a military campaign. San Martín thought all this political business a thing for pettifogging lawyers, and he distrusted Bolívar as an intellectual rather than a soldier. Compared with San Martín, indeed, Bolívar might have been considered an amateur, while San Martín had been brought up from the beginning as a regular soldier. He had formed an army on the European model, and trained it to fight according to the text-books. Even his expedition across the Andes was a conquest according to rule, as his friend Sarmiento said. But if, like Bolívar, he had had to lead irregular troops, be defeated in one place and then appear unexpectedly in another, he would never have been quick enough. In that sense Bolívar was far more American than San Martín; and he was essentially American, too, in his distrust of crowned heads. San Martín's position in Peru was already rather uncertain. He apparently did not know that the moment his back was turned a movement against him had broken out in Lima; and it was only when Bolívar showed him a letter from the Secretary of the Colombian Legation in Peru, describing what had happened, that San Martín realized that there was nothing more he could do but retire from public life.

> "San Martín," Mosquera says, "read the letter which the Liberator gave him, took a note of it and said: 'If this is so, my public life is over. I shall leave my native land, go to Europe, and spend the rest of my life in retirement; and I only hope that before I die I shall be able to welcome the triumph of those republican principles which you defend. Time and events will tell which of us two has foreseen the future most clearly.'
>
> "The Liberator answered: 'Neither we nor the generation which comes after us will see the splendour of the Republic which we are founding now. I regard South America as being in the chrysalis stage. There will be a metamorphosis in the physical condition of the inhabitants; and in the end there will be a new people, a blend of all the races composing it, which will produce homogeneity. Let us not retard the progress of the human race with institutions which, as I said, are exotic on the virgin soil of South America.' "

Agreement was impossible. If the Protector would not give way to the Liberator on the question of monarchy, the Liberator was unlikely to give any real military aid to Peru. San Martín, though he could not understand Bolívar's objections to monarchy, understood very well what the military situation in Peru would be, if he had to go on fighting the Spaniards without Bolívar's Colombians to help him. It was a situation which he could not face. He left Guayaquil at once; and on his return to Lima resigned his command and the office of president, and retired into private life. He came to Europe, and settled with his daughter near Fontainebleau, where he lived in modest circumstances until the middle of the nineteenth century. It was a noble and generous act of renunciation. San Martín was certainly mortified at the result of the meeting at Guayaquil, and seldom referred to it, even to imitate South American friends. Indeed, he eventually came to deny that he had ever thought of setting up a monarchy in the New World. But the cause of his failure is clear: his monarchist ideas in a continent which, for better or worse, has remained firmly republican.

On San Martín's retirement, Bolívar immediately sent two battalions to strengthen the Peruvian army. To his surprise, the new government declined them with thanks, and returned them to Guayaquil. But when, at the beginning of 1823, the Peruvians suffered two heavy reverses from the Spaniards, they made haste to apply to Bolívar again, with the most humble excuses.

Bolívar hastened to send more troops; and he also sent Sucre—the best and most loyal of his generals. Then, in September 1823, when he had received formal permission from the Colombian Congress, Bolívar went down to Peru himself. The situation was discouraging. The Peruvian military leaders were all at sixes and sevens, while the Spanish Viceroy had an army of 14,000 men; finally the President of the Peruvian Republic, the Vice-President and the Minister of War all went over to the Spaniards. Worst of all, Bolívar, on whom the Peruvian Congress had conferred supreme political and military powers, was overcome by the climate and fell seriously ill. As soon as he could get up, he set about reorganizing the army. The campaign in Peru offered some of the greatest difficulties he had ever faced; but on 2nd August, 1823, he was able to review 7,700 men at Cerro de Pasco, 14,000 ft. up in the Andes.

> "Men," he said to them, "the enemy you are going to destroy boasts that he has been winning for 14 years. So he is worthy of measuring his arms against yours, which have also shone brilliantly in a great number of engagements."

In a fantastic setting of high mountains and big lakes, Bolívar fought a great cavalry battle. It was at Junín, on 7th August, 1823: "a very sharp affair of cavalry," an English officer called it, and the British had good reason to know how sharp an affair it was. The combatants were chiefly hussars and lancers. No fire-arms were used by either side; and except for the sound of hoofs on the plain, and the hoarse shouts of the men engaged, the battle was fought in silence—in a landscape more like the mountains of the moon than an earthly battlefield. In under an hour the Spanish cavalry were broken and dispersed; Bolívar's men had the measure of their enemies.

Four months later they met again (9th December, 1824) at Ayacucho. Bolívar was down at Lima this time, Acting-President of the Peruvian Republic. He had given the command to Sucre, the Colombian Congress having made a ruling that the Liberator (who was also, at that time, President of the Colombian Union) could not act as the head of another state—Peru—and at the same time command a Colombian army in the field. It was a mere quibble, but he obeyed.

After four arduous months of marching and counter-marching, the two armies met near Ayacucho, a place on the road between Lima and Cuzco, 9,200 ft. above the sea. The Royalists were considerably stronger than the Republicans, who now included detachments from all parts of South America (9,310 against 5,780); but the viceroy was out-manœuvred and out-matched by the brilliant generalship of Sucre, and suffered an overwhelming defeat.

Ayacucho was the end of Spanish power in South America. The Viceroy was captured, and many senior officers. They were allowed a free passage back to Spain, and liberty to dispose of their personal property in Peru; but all arms, ammunition and stores were to be handed over. The Spanish commandant of the port of Callao, General Rodil, refused to accept these surprisingly generous terms, and quixotically held out for a year longer (until 2nd January, 1826) when he too surrendered.

Bolívar was in his office in Lima when the news of Ayacucho came in. He tore off his tunic, and stamped on it. "Thank God," he exclaimed, "I shall never have to command any more!"

Chapter Eight

"Emperor of the Andes"

AYACUCHO was the greatest moment of Bolívar's life. The Peruvian campaign was over; the independence of the last and oldest Spanish dominion had been finally won. The international army which Bolívar had built up had not failed him in his absence, and the commander whom he had inspired and trained had shown the loyalty and devotion expected of him. "Above all," Sucre wrote after the battle, " I am happy to have complied with your orders. This letter is badly written, and the ideas are confused. But in itself, it is worth something: it brings the news of a great victory and the liberation of Peru. As a reward, I only ask you to keep your friendship for me."

Bolívar summoned Congress. It voted him dictatorial powers which he did not want, and a million pesos which he declined. They talked of statues, medals, memorial inscriptions. At last Bolívar, who had spent most of his private fortune in public works, and freed a thousand slaves who were legally his property, suggested that the million might be given for charitable purposes in the towns of the Colombian Union. It was never paid.

The Liberator spent the first eight months of his dictatorship travelling through the different provinces of Peru, inquiring into local government, opening schools, and trying to improve the conditions of the Indians. Some municipalities were readier with their gifts than with their reforms; at Arequipa, at the foot of a snow-capped volcano, they presented him with a fine horse, the bit, stirrups and other metal-work of solid gold. From Cuzco, the ancient Inca capital, 11,500 ft. above the sea, he moved south-east to Puno, a thousand feet higher, on the shore of the great inland lake of Titicaca, site of the earliest Peruvian civilization. He sailed over the lake (which is more than 100 miles long) in one of the peculiar Indian *balsas*, rafts made of reeds; and then rode to La Paz, the modern capital of Bolivia, to Chuquisaca, the ancient Indian capital, and to Potosí with the famous mountain made entirely of silver.

All these places are in the modern state of Bolivia, named after Bolívar himself; but originally they formed part of the provinces of Upper Peru (Alto Perú), and had later been transferred to the Viceroyalty of La Plata. La Paz had actually been the first town in South America to begin the revolution against the Spanish Government; on 16th July, 1809, an "open council" (*cabildo abierto*) had deposed the Spanish authorities and formed a *junta* of its own. But they were unlucky; their *junta* was suppressed, and they only secured definite independence after Ayacucho, when the assembly of Upper Peru founded a republic, named it after the Liberator, elected him president and asked him to draw up a constitution for them. Bolívar appointed Marshal Sucre his substitute—he had been promoted Field-Marshal after Ayacucho—and rode down to Lima.

The constitution that he sent them is not merely one more example of romantic constitution-making, it is among the Liberator's most important political pronouncements. The Bolivian Assembly adopted it with slight modifications, the most noticeable being the article referring to the new republic's religion, which Bolívar had left open but which the Assembly declared to be Roman Catholic to the exclusion of all others. Bolívar had deliberately refrained from laying down what the religion of the state should be, as he had in his earlier constitution for Angostura. He regarded a constitution as a guarantee of civil and political rights; its only concern with religion was to safeguard a man's right to practise the religion dictated by his conscience. To establish religion by law was to stultify it; for by imposing necessity upon duty it removed all meaning from faith, upon which all religion rested. It was a moral question, not a political one.

> "Should the State rule the conscience of its subjects?" he asked; "watch over the fulfilment of religious laws and decree rewards and punishments in matters of faith? The tribun-

> als for that were in heaven, and God was the judge. Only the Inquisition could act for them in this world; but was a modern State to restore the Inquisition and burnings at the stake?"

Bolívar's constitution for Bolivia, like the earlier one for Angostura, is a document of the greatest interest; and though it proved unworkable after a few years' trial, it is still among the most notable American contributions to political thought. At Angostura, in 1819, he had been fascinated by the constitutional practice of Britain; his Bolivian Constitution seems rather to be influenced by the First Consulate in France. Again, at Angostura, Bolívar had been little more than the commander of partisan Republican troops engaged in desultory warfare against the Spanish Royalists, with a capital which he had only just occupied and a congress which, as a rule, merely approved what he had already done. So he could formulate his political theories pretty much as he fancied, keeping an eye on the monarchical susceptibilities of Europe. But by 1826, many things had changed. Bolívar in Peru was no longer so free as he had been at Angostura.

According to the new constitution the supreme power was divided into four branches instead of three: the electoral body; the legislative (i.e. Congress); the executive (the President), and the judiciary (the law courts). Electoral power was vested in all male Bolivian citizens over 21. They must be able to read and write—a requirement which defranchised all the Indians and many of the half-breeds—and they must not be in servitude to another; besides granting religious liberty, the Bolivian Constitution abolished slavery. The franchise required no property-qualification, or the need to possess private means. "The exercise of public power," Bolívar wrote, "demands knowledge and honesty—not money." Every four years the citizens were to choose an electoral body, one elector for every ten citizens—a plan which has been traced to the Napoleonic constitutions of the years VIII and IX. This body elected the legislative assembly, including provincial governors and subordinate officials: prefects, mayors, magistrates, senators and parish priests. Congress consisted of three chambers instead of two: tribunes, senators and censors. "It takes two to make a quarrel," Bolívar implied, "but a third can generally make peace." He rejected the single-chamber government proposed in France by Sièyes. Tribunes and senators were to be elected for periods of four and eight years respectively, but the censors were elected for life. They were to exercise the political and moral power which Bolívar had proposed at Angostura.

Executive power was vested in the President, assisted by three secretaries of state; it was a life-appointment and carried with it the power of nominating a successor. "The authority of the President must be perpetual," Bolívar declared, "because in countries with no social distinctions, it is necessary to have some fixed point around which everything revolves." But as a check on tyranny, the life-president was deprived of all direct influence; he did not make either judicial or ecclesiastical appointments. The president-for-life is foreshadowed in the Jamaica letter, while in the Constitution of Angostura there is a president with a long term of office and with the door left open for a life-appointment. The Colombian Union had in its constitution a life-term president in the place of an English constitutional monarch; but Bolivia had a Napoleonic life-term Consul, with power to nominate the man who succeeded him. Bolívar did not admit where his model came from; rather than name Napoleon, he preferred to give the credit to Petion, the life-president of Haiti, who had helped him in his difficulties in 1815. He was careful to spread abroad the idea that a life-presidency would not lead eventually to monarchy. A restoration was impossible in America, he said; no king could endure without great nobles and high dignitaries of the church.

Bolívar's four powers in the State have been compared with the five proposed for the restored French monarchy by Benjamin Constant. Both were seeking a firm foundation for liberty; and Constant wished to add a fifth power to the four proposed by Montesquieu, and divide the government into legislative, royal, executive, judiciary and municipal branches. Bolívar conceived public power in a more complete and exact form. He divided it into four branches: the three already recognized, and an electoral power as well. He too hoped that his plan for the Bolivian Constitution might be a source of union and firmness to South American governments. It was, he claimed, as popular as any other; and by the importance it attached to the electoral bodies, it conferred sovereignty on the people in the act on which popular sovereignty most immediately depended: casting their votes. With its life-president it should be strong enough and steady enough to resist the jolts and jars and sudden oscillations to which a new state was subject. In no other representative government was there so much popular liberty, he declared, so much direct intervention by the citizens themselves, and so much power in the president. It combined a just presentation of the federal system, the solidity of a centralized administration and the stability of a monarchy. The Bolivian Constitution had, in fact, all the advantages of a limited monarchy and a republic: "a throne draped in republican colours," a French diplomat described it. "The colours," he added, "are an illusion; but Bolívar thinks that all his glory comes from them." The truth was that the new constitution did not suit the social conditions of the peoples for whom it was intended; in the end they were to sacrifice all hope of peace and prosperity to the personal ambition of various *caudillos* and become involved in a succession of civil wars. "The fate of the Bolivian Constitution," the historian Gil Fortoul remarks, "was to be the same as that of many other Latin American constitutions: it ended in tumult and was replaced by one which turned out to be worse."

The first life-president to be appointed was Sucre; but he accepted only on condition that he might, if he wished, be allowed to resign after two years. His rule was "enlightened, progressive, liberal—and weak."

Meanwhile domestic disturbances in Colombia (1826) obliged the Liberator to return from Peru. His presence seemed necessary everywhere to inspire that loyalty and common sense without which his schemes would not work; and not even Bolívar himself was able to prevent the eventual dissolution of the Colombian Union into its original components. In spite of 300 years of Spanish colonial government, each viceroyalty, captaincy-general or presidency had become a foreign country to its next-door neighbour, and hopes of union between Spanish-speaking countries were already remote.

To many observers, particularly in London, the chief difficulties of the Colombian Union were financial. The six per cent. loans had been eagerly taken up when first issued; but the Colombian Government had never been able to make regular payments of the interest, and the Colombian and Venezuelan representatives sent to London were either too inexperienced in financial matters to inspire confidence, or had not sufficient command of the English language to maintain it. Many of them—such, for instance, as Francisco Zea—were men of unblemished integrity; but in money matters they were incompetent, and sometimes found themselves in gaol for debt. In Colombia it was necessary to maintain a comparatively large standing army, in case Spain might renew the war, or disturbances break out at home; and that condition made demands on the treasury which prolonged the precarious state of the national finances of the countries composing the Colombian Union until after the Union broke up. Andrés Bello, Bolívar's former tutor, now secretary of the Colombian Legation in London, wrote to Bolívar on 21st March, 1827:

"One thing deserves your attention above all others, and that is the public credit of Colombia. On the other side of the Atlantic, perhaps, it is not so clear as it is here how impossible it is to raise another loan in London. I say impossible, because if anything were arranged now, the sacrifice would be enormous, and our government would be obliged to negotiate with speculators of doubtful character. But even if we were able to shut our eyes to everything in order to raise another loan, Your Excellency knows very well that by this means we should not restore our credit, but lower it even more . . . Believe me, the proposal would produce the most unfortunate impression in London against our government; on the contrary, one of the methods most likely to conciliate the good will of these people who are so influential in the world, is the religious payment of all obligations contracted."

In 1829, Bolívar's A.D.C., Belford Wilson, wrote in the same sense: the technique of alternate defaults and funding loans was already beginning to wear thin.

As soon as Bolívar reached Lima on his return from the south (10th February, 1826) he sent for the British Consul-General and had a long conversation with him. Historians have perhaps been too greatly concerned with Bolívar's attitude towards monarchy. In North and South America his supposedly monarchist leanings had bred suspicion, while in England—both to statesmen of the time and to historians since—the Liberator's understanding of monarchy has hardly seemed to go far enough. The most interesting side to Bolívar's view is its friendliness to Britain. His admiration for British institutions and British policies has never been sufficiently appreciated. There can be no doubt of his genuineness, and he infected his diplomatic agents abroad with something of his own enthusiasm. In the House of Lords he was described as the basis of the union which gave support and security to the liberty of South America.

Affable to foreigners, and particularly to foreign

diplomats, admirer of North American idealism and still more of the French way of life, Bolívar gave all who saw him the impression that he understood their anxieties and would never offend their susceptibilities. Yet, taking all his pronouncements into consideration, the conclusion of a Venezuelan historian is that "in spite of his Spanish soul and his French culture, he would have given his America—if he could—the institutions, the character and the political virtues of the people of England." British support was one of the things which Bolívar most earnestly desired; and he took particular trouble to adapt his conversation to English officials, and to make it clear to any British representative he met that he was not a "red republican." He had, he insinuated, no objection to monarchy in the abstract; he did not mind monarchies in other places, provided there were no attempt to introduce them into South America. There was, it was true, an Emperor in Brazil, and there had been an Emperor in Mexico; but one crowned head in the New World was enough. America was not meant for monarchy.

British officials were agreeably surprised. What attracted them to Bolívar was not so much his very real admiration and friendliness for Britain; his ideas of a life-president seemed to naval men and consular officials hardly republican at all. They begin their reports guardedly enough, with reference to "a foreign commander of a foreign force." That is how the Liberator is first described by Thomas Rowcroft, British Consul-General at Lima, in a letter to Canning (19th July, 1824); and he refers in a supercilious manner to "the war which General Bolívar is supposed here to be carrying on against the person who considers himself to be the Viceroy of the King of Spain." He sent formal notice of his arrival to Bolívar, who was at Huancayo, up in the Andes, with his troops. He enclosed a copy of the *Polignac Memorandum*: the account of a conversation which had taken place in the spring of 1823 between Canning and the French Ambassador in London, the Prince de Polignac, when the latter had given an assurance that French forces would not be used against the new states in America to support any attempt of the Spanish Crown to recover them.

This document, which showed so clearly the intentions of the British Government with regard to the future of South America, and the stand made by Britain for independence, is now believed to have done more to keep European powers from intervention than the famous declaration of President Monroe known as the "Monroe Doctrine." It is worth quoting some of the original words of the presidential declaration, for comparison :

"The occasion has been judged proper for asserting . . . that the American Continents, by the free and independent condition which they have assumed and maintain, are henceforth not to be considered as subjects for future colonisation by any European powers. . . . We should consider any attempt on their part to extend their system to any portion of this hemisphere as dangerous to our peace and safety."

President Monroe's message was published first (2nd December, 1823); but the conversation to which the Polignac memorandum refers, though not published until March 1824, had already taken place when the President's declaration was made, and Canning had even suggested (in August 1823) that a joint declaration against European intervention in America should be made by Britain and the United States. This was refused on the ground that the United States and Great Britain were not on the same level. The United States had already recognized (1822) the independent governments of La Plata, Chile, Peru, Colombia and Mexico, while Britain had not. There could be no joint declaration, because Britain and the United States had not the same standing in the matter. Canning did not see the point; but John Quincey Adams saw the United States' opportunity, and the presidential declaration of the Monroe Doctrine was the result. The occasion had indeed "been judged proper." At the time, the declaration meant little; its full implications were not apparent. It was only later that, by a famous irony, the Monroe Doctrine was made to stink in the nostrils of the very peoples for whose protection it had been formulated. That was in 1889, when pan-Americanism became a "diplomatic trade-mark" (as it was called) for United States exports; and when President Theodore Roosevelt assumed, as a corollary to the Monroe Doctrine, the right to forestall European occupation by taking charge of the collection of American debts to European creditors.

As a matter of fact British policy had for many years been moving in the direction of non-intervention, as the history of British recognition of South American independence shows. What Britain really wanted was the right to trade, and British governments were on the watch for any action from any other European power which might interfere with their trading privileges. British command of the sea was absolute. No fleet could move against Latin America unless Britain allowed it to pass; indeed it could be only by the help or connivance of the British Navy that Spain could have re-established her empire. Bolívar gratefully acknowledged the fact, in a letter of 1823:

> "Only England, mistress of the seas, can protect us against the united forces of European reaction."

British statesmen were, of course, led mainly by motives of self-interest, which is ultimately "the determining factor in the policy of all nations." But on the side of Bolívar and the armies of liberation there were powerful currents of English opinion; and when it became known that Ferdinand VII had re-established the Spanish Inquisition, his absolutist and persecuting government became extremely unpopular in this country. That feeling, like the indignation expressed by Wordsworth at the Convention of Cintra in 1808, or—to take a modern instance—the disgust felt by opinion in Britain at the official British treatment of the Spanish Republic after 1936—was altogether apart from the commercial and other interests which decide foreign policy and eventually dictate it. Public opinion in England in the time of Bolívar had more in common with the visionary justice of Byron and Shelley than with the cool calculations of Castlereagh and Canning; and this opinion was strengthened by the feeling which found conspicuous expression in the movement in favour of the abolition of slavery: a feeling which was stoutly protestant, and liberal.

In 1813 Britain had protested at the expedition of Morillo, and Castlereagh saw that the former Spanish colonies must be given self-government, if only that they might trade freely with the rest of the world. In 1817 he favoured British mediation between Spain and the former colonies. Spain refused to agree to the terms, and at the moment nothing could be done. Yet Castlereagh had made the independence of Spanish America a foregone conclusion. In 1822, when the United States recognized Colombia, the Colombian Government threatened to close their ports to the shipping of all other countries. British merchants were greatly alarmed; there were protests, and a petition from the City urged that some kind of recognition was essential. Castlereagh accordingly recognized the flags of South American ships—an act which amounted to recognition *de facto* of their governments.

Canning's interest in Latin America was also due to its importance to British trade; he began by sending out Consular agents. He failed to stop the French from invading Spain in 1823, and the isolation of Britain which followed made him turn to the United States. This approach, coming just at that moment, removed the last American fears of European intervention, and so provided the opportunity for the declaration of the Monroe Doctrine. Yet so far as the Latin American countries were concerned, the main point was already won before the publication of President Monroe's message. Canning had obtained, in the interview with Polignac, "an avowal that force would not be used against the new states," and his agents in South America used it with great effect to show that Britain had been first to protest against attack from Europe. The result was that when at last British recognition came, it seemed to the Latin American peoples to be of far greater importance than recognition by the

United States. The method of recognition adopted was to negotiate commercial treaties.

Such was the background of Mr. Thomas Rowcroft, and the communication which he sent up to Bolívar in the Andes. The Consul-General's letter had been delivered by Lieutenant Kelly, R.N., of H.M.S. *Cambridge*, sent by the senior British officer commanding on the station, Captain Maling. Kelly found Bolívar "much pleased by the attention shown to him, greatly attached to the British and much prejudiced against the United States and the French." The war seemed to be going well; the Liberator found "more difficulty to get over the country and to get at the enemy than to fight him"; but this was only natural "in a country of hills and rocks and sands, without roads, rivers, canals or wheels."

Later on Captain Maling himself had a conversation with Bolívar. It was duly reported to the Foreign Office; but the comment was that perhaps "Captain Maling did not fully embrace what he could have desired." He made the Liberator seem so monarchist and anti-democratic that he was probably expressing his own feelings rather than the ideas which Bolívar had expressed to him.

C. M. Ricketts, a later Consul-General in Peru, writing to Canning on 18th February, 1826, makes Bolívar more guarded. Perhaps he understood him better than Captain Maling did, for they conversed "in the French language, which he speaks very fluently."

"He had nothing to do, as a public character, with any of the European systems, though he might respect some more than others, and he most assuredly did not at this juncture uphold a Republican form of government as superior to any other, for he was aware that with imperfect materials it might be despotic or tyrannical. All he had sought was freedom from Spain, as the South Americans felt that they were sufficiently strong to throw off the foreign rule and to govern themselves. . . . Circumstances might vary the form, and an Emperor should not be objected to in Brazil nor a Federal Government in the sister state of Buenos Aires; but he had his notion for the Government of Colombia, and other forms again for Upper and Lower Peru."

"These were the sentiments," he added, "which he had wished Captain Maling to convey to you."

"At that moment he was impressed with an apprehension owing to a French squadron coming suddenly to these seas, that the Allied Sovereigns were preparing to coalesce with Spain under the false conception that a radical spirit was raised in South America which would not rest until after their ascendancy had ceased."

He did not consider a federal system of government to be the one best calculated for "these infant states," as "the minds of the people were not yet prepared to take a leading part in the administration of public affairs." The United States was a solitary instance of a nation uniting and at once establishing a Federal State without anarchy and on a just and solid basis. In South America, on the contrary, the inhabitants had just emerged from a state of slavery; and to expect good order and honesty from such materials was absurd. Some governments—he mentioned particularly that of Buenos Aires—had endeavoured to counteract that result; but unfortunately each province was so busy discussing liberty, justice and national rights, that:

> "although few of them could read, each had its own Sancho for a governor . . . and all thought because they spoke of liberty, that they were free and wise, and because they had armed a small force, that they had become one among the powerful and well-regulated nations of this earth."

Bolívar added that his own principle was to encourage education and industry, and to issue rules and laws founded on the plainest and most simple principles, for which he should take as his guide the civil "Code Napoleon," the only wise thing, he thought, that Buonaparte ever did. He was certainly anxious for British support; he needed it for the realization of one of his greatest projects; the international American congress at

Panamá. But Bolívar was always difficult for European officials to understand. He seemed to them a mass of paradox: a revolutionary general who was not on the make, and could even resist the temptation to make himself an emperor.

Chapter Nine

The Panamá Congress

THE idea of British support for an international congress and a league of South American nations was not a mere happy thought of Bolívar's, a sudden improvisation. It had occupied his mind ever since the beginning of the Colombian Union. Bolívar was not one of those Spanish generals, of the familiar nineteenth- or twentieth-century pattern, who come forward as the saviours of their country, win one or two battles (with or without foreign intervention) and assume dictatorial powers. Bolívar was a man of very different mould: a visionary, an intellectual. He saw farther, and wished to provide for the future of the whole of Spanish-speaking America. He had been thinking along these lines for many years, even before he had liberated Peru and founded Bolivia.

It has been claimed that the original inspiration came from Miranda; but its practical development is already to be seen in an article which Bolívar wrote for the London *Morning Chronicle* (5th September, 1810), saying that if the Venezuelans were obliged to declare war on Spain, they would invite all the peoples of America to join them in a confederation. The plan appears again in Bolívar's Cartagena manifesto (1812), and more definitely in 1814, when, as liberator of Venezuela, he sent out the circular which made the freedom of the new states conditional on what he called "the union of the whole of South America in one body politic." In the Letter from Jamaica (1815) he saw clearly the need for an international congress, with all the Spanish-speaking American nations united in a great confederation; and in 1818, replying to the message of greeting sent to Angostura by the Argentine "director," Pueyrredón, he said that as soon as the war of independence was over he would hasten to form an American pact, and he hoped—vainly, as it turned out—that the River Plate Provinces would join him. The *patria*, the nationality, should be one and the same for all Spanish-speaking Americans; their motto should be the unity of South America. From Chile, too, O'Higgins had suggested the idea of an American confederation; while San Martín, in a proclamation to the inhabitants of Peru in 1818, had advised the closer union of Argentina, Chile and Peru for military reasons.

When Bolívar's reconquest had advanced far enough for him to send diplomatic agents to the other countries and draw up instructions for them, the scope and duties of an international American congress were clear in his mind.

"It should be a league that is truly American, not formed merely on the principles of an ordinary alliance for offence and defence. It should be stricter than the league which has been formed lately in Europe against popular liberties [the so-called 'Holy' Alliance between Austria, Russia and Prussia]. . . . Ours must be a society of sister nations, united, strong, and capable of withstanding the aggression of foreign powers."

It should be an Amphictyonic League[1]—Bolívar was thinking of the Amphictyonic League of the twelve leading states of ancient Greece—an assembly of plenipotentiaries to discuss matters of common interest to all the Spanish-speaking American states; and it should be prepared to resolve—by arbitration—any discords which might arise between them.

To take an example: a frequent cause of dispute in South America has arisen from international boundaries. Bolívar's envoys, whether in America or Europe, were instructed to act on the principle already mentioned, that the boundaries of the succession states (after emancipation from Spain) should follow the boundaries formerly existing between the various viceroyalties, captaincies-general and presidencies of the old Spanish Empire—that is, the boundaries as they were in 1810. This principle has been of great practical importance. Bolívar may not

[1] The term means " a league of good neighbours."

have foreseen all its difficulties: those, for instance, which arose in the boundary dispute between Venezuela and Great Britain in 1895; but he recommended that they should be settled by arbitration.

Bolívar hoped to achieve, through his international congress, a solemn pact of union between the Spanish-speaking American nations. But there were difficulties, and they sprang up on all sides. The first difficulty came from the River Plate; and the River Plate Government had a point of view of its own. It is important to understand the Argentine position and to realize why it is different from that of other South American countries, particularly those in the north. It is a position which is more readily appreciated in England than that of the more northern Spanish American countries; but it is not necessarily the only position, nor is a writer impartial because he accepts it. In the present instance, the Government of Buenos Aires felt unable to do more than sign a treaty of friendship, and enter into a defensive alliance with Colombia. Separated by geographical barriers and economic ideals from the more northerly Spanish-speaking republics, it declined to accept treaties already negotiated by the Colombian Government with Chile or Peru. Rivadavia, who had succeeded Pueyrredón as head of the Government of Buenos Aires, rejected the idea of a congress to arbitrate on international questions. He thought it a useless and dangerous imitation of an institution of ancient Greece. He distrusted arbitration—so did statesmen in Europe—and seeing few signs of danger at that time (1823) he was of opinion that entangling alliances with other South American states would serve no useful purpose. Yet as soon as Brazil began to look dangerous over the *Banda Oriental* (the future Uruguay), he at once begged for an alliance with Colombia and Peru. His vision may have been distorted by other causes; he was one of those who were hoping to see a European prince reigning some day in Buenos Aires, and had little sympathy with the republican idealism of Bolívar.

Difficulties of a different kind—or, rather, misunderstandings due to other causes—came from the United States. The States were still glowing with their own liberation from England; they had been quick to recognize the new Latin American nations in 1822, before Britain had done so; but they did not pay Bolívar all the attention he deserved and favoured his schemes more in theory than in practice. In Washington, Bolívar's plans for pan-American union seemed to be aimed chiefly at the military union of South America against Spain; but the need for that would cease, it was thought, when the full effects of President Monroe's declaration were felt. The specific objects of the Panamá Congress: "the establishment of close and cordial relations, commercial intercourse, the interchange of political thought, and the habits of good understanding between the new republics and the United States," might perhaps be attained by a meeting at Panamá such as Bolívar desired. The United States administration of the day had not the full support of the country, and on this occasion the United States lost the opportunity. It was admitted afterwards that "the new states were removed from the sympathy and protecting influence of our [i.e. United States] example, and their commerce which we might then have secured passed into other [i.e. British] hands." "The earnest and patriotic Colombians (as the document describes them) failed to crystallize a truly American system for the American continent."

The idea of a congress to secure the union of Spanish America against Spain was as old as the idea of independence; but from the first it met with great difficulties. Some of them have already been described; others were due to the enormous distances between the new states. Bolívar dreamed of a Latin American "union, league and perpetual federation"; and though nothing came of it at the time, it is hard to realize what a stupendous notion had entered Bolívar's head. He thought of federating a string of countries as long as from Archangel to Zanzibar, and separated by enormous physical barriers. Even now, travelling salesmen sometimes forget that communications are scanty and that goods must be packed small. A recent writer from the United States heard Latin American customers exclaim: "*Señor*, for God's sake send me nothing that can't be carried by two men and a mule!" Two men and a mule could never have carried Bolívar's perpetual federation up the Orinoco and over the Andes. Continental policies needed vision—which Bolívar had, but they also needed roads, rails, wires, pipes and planes. Before it could achieve much, Bolívar's pan-Americanism had to become, in the literal sense, a winged word.

It was only when he became president of the Colombian Union, in 1821, that he made contact between the north of the continent and the south, sending envoys to Mexico and Buenos Aires, Chile and Peru. The preparatory stages of the congress which he proposed to hold at Panamá were a series of treaties between the Colombian Union and the other states of Spanish-speaking America. They contained provisions for defending their independence against Spain or any other foreign power, a meeting of accredited representatives of the several nations, and a recommendation that they should use their good offices with the governments of other states of the former Spanish Empire to enter into a pact of union, league and perpetual federation, and that this should be followed by a general congress of plenipotentiaries. This congress was to serve (in Bolívar's words) as:

"a council in conflict, a means of contact in common danger, a faithful interpreter of public treaties when interpretation was needed, and a judge, arbiter, and mediator in differences and disputes."

Bolívar naturally informed Britain of his schemes. He looked to Britain in particular, as a friend of justice and liberty; and hoped that Canning would send a representative to the Congress. In fact, Bolívar's vision of pan-Americanism differed from all later ones, because it treated Britain as an American power, and on this occasion it was Canning's vision which proved to be short-sighted.

We may wonder why Canning should have viewed the proposals—particularly those for arbitration and a league of South American nations—with comparative coolness. One of his reasons was the fear—the obsession, it almost seems now—of a republic. One must remember that 120 years ago the experiences of European statesmen with republicanism, as it had worked out in France, were not encouraging; while in Spain the Cortes of Cadiz, though it was acting as a regency for "His Captive Majesty," Ferdinand VII, showed quite clearly that Spaniards could live without a king, and had thoroughly alarmed British statesmen by its liberalism. In 1823, barely ten years after the Duke of Wellington had laboriously driven the French from one end of Spain to the other, a royalist French army had occupied Spain once more to defend the Spanish monarchy from the "extravagant liberalism" of the constitution which Ferdinand had been obliged to restore in 1820. This was the army which the Spanish novelist Pérez Galdós has described in the title of one of his *Episodios nacionales*, "The hundred thousand sons of St. Louis": an army of French crusaders, conjured up by the romantic imagination of Chateaubriand to defend church and king against Spanish republicanism. Canning and his agents in South America thought it would be a good thing "if all the new states in South America could be monarchies, like Brazil." A republic still seemed suspicious and hardly respectable, and the question of British participation in the Congress of Panamá came somehow to be involved with the question of monarchy.

Canning did not go so far as to approve the plan (which had actually been suggested) of placing the new states under British protection. The phrase "South America is ours," let slip in one of his letters, is to be taken in the sense of trade. He declared, however, in his instructions to the observer sent to the Panamá Congress, that Britain would not object to a "League of states, lately colonies of Spain, growing out of their common relations in Spain." He saw its advantages to Britain; but he insisted that any project for putting the United States at the head of an American confederation as against Europe would be highly displeasing to His Majesty's Government. The result of a confederation, he cynically foresaw, would be the division of the new states into hostile groups, and Canning's policy aimed at maintaining harmonious relations with them all. He was particularly anxious for a friendly settlement of the differences between Buenos Aires and Brazil, while keeping Bolívar from intervening in the quarrel between the two countries. Again, nothing should interrupt the friendly relations then existing between Britain and the United States. So he rejected the overtures made by the Colombian Minister in London; "he feared," Bolívar was informed, "that the rest of the nations will view the league unfavourably, and particularly the United States." Canning was right.

By the end of 1824, Bolívar was pressing for the Congress of Panamá to meet as soon as possible. Bolívar was right, too. One of the reasons why the Congress was ineffective was that it met too late, when the first flush of enthusiasm was over, and the attitude of many people in the newly freed Spanish American States had become less idealist. "If we wait any longer," he said, "if we wait and see what the others are going to do, we deprive them of the advantages which the assembly would give them from the very day of its opening." In other words, if the other republics did not make up their minds at once, he foresaw that they might miss their opportunities.

Unfortunately, it took nearly two years of negotiation before the First Panamá Congress met (22nd June, 1826); and then only a few countries were represented: Colombia, Central America, Mexico and Peru. Among the absentees, Chile, in spite of promises made earlier, appointed its delegates too late. From Bolivia President Sucre sent blank credentials, asking the Liberator to fill them in; Bolivia was not represented. The government of the River Plate Provinces abstained. So also did Brazil, saying that the Emperor was neutral between what he termed "the belligerent States of South America" and Spain. The United States also pleaded neutrality on account of an expedition which Colombia was preparing (with Bolívar's encouragement) for the liberation of Cuba and Puerto Rico. When at last it was known that the Colombian expedition would not sail, it was too late for the representatives of the United States to reach Panamá in time. Congress had appointed the U.S. Minister at Bogotá (who died on the journey to the Isthmus) and another delegate who only reached Panamá when the meetings were over. Even if they had arrived in time, they would have made difficulties, for their instructions differed widely from the ideas of Bolívar. The United States Secretary of State, Clay, would not accept the idea of an international council with powers of deciding controversies between American states, or in any way influencing their conduct. He did not like the idea of arbitration, and would have preferred a simple, common declaration from the Spanish American states, in conformity with the Monroe Doctrine, that "within the boundaries of their respective territories they would not permit the establishment of new European colonies." He would have liked at the same time—and here Canning would have supported him—a joint declaration in favour of religious liberty and toleration of other confessions than the Roman Catholic.

Britain and Holland sent observers. Bolívar had hoped that Britain might have done more than send "a silent witness of the discussions." He was aware, he told the British Consul-General in Peru, of the generous policy which had moved Canning to seek no benefit beyond what other European powers might possess; but in fact the weight and influence of Britain already preponderated, through her command of the sea, her "generous, friendly and steady procedure," by the capital advanced and the industry introduced by British subjects.

Canning's instructions to the British observer, E. J. Dawkins, give a very clear insight into what he thought British policy on the American Continent should be. It should be remembered that Canning was never very partial to the United States. His famous phrase, about calling the New World into existence to right the balance of the Old, had been used before by Bolívar, in his letter from Jamaica; and what Canning had in mind was calling into existence an independent South America to redress the balance of the North. So the observer, Mr. Dawkins, was instructed to collect the views and policies of the various American governments, their feelings towards one another, and more especially the amount of influence in their concerns which they seemed likely to tolerate from the United States.

> To a league among the States lately colonies of Spain, limited to objects growing out of their common relation to Spain, His Majesty's Government would not object. But any project for putting the United States at the head of an American Confederacy as against Europe would be highly displeasing.

Among the objects of the Congress Canning had noticed that of being "a faithful interpreter of publick treaties" and "an arbitrator and conciliator in disputes and differences." To the principle of arbitration—Bolívar's greatest contribution to peace and international law—Canning paid less attention than to the possibility of the Panamá Congress becoming what he called "a species of league of Americans against Europe." "It can hardly be apprehended," he went on, "that the function of 'interpreting publick treaties' can be pretended to be assumed by any assembly with respect to any other than its own members."

States which had a common relation to Spain, and a common interest in the maintenance of the freedom which they had asserted, might consent among themselves to a general, corporate superintendence of their respective engagements with one another.

> "But we do not understand it to be intended, nor could we admit, that this superintendence should extend further; that a treaty concluded by one of the Spanish American states with another power (by Colombia, for instance, with Buenos Aires, or Mexico with Great Britain) should be submitted to the 'interpretation' of the Congress of Panamá."

Canning also desired Dawkins to express the opinion of his government on the establishment of peace between the states of Spanish America and Spain. The only temptation, he acidly remarked, for Spain to recognize the independence of the new American states would be "the prospect afforded to His Catholic Majesty of some relief for his pecuniary embarrassments." At an earlier period of the wars of independence, the notion of buying the recognition of Spain by a money payment from the revolted colonies had occurred to him; and a treaty had even been concluded by Buenos Aires agreeing to the purchase of recognition. Canning saw one awkward contingency, however: funds derived from one of the new states for the recognition of their independence might be used by the mother country in fitting out expeditions to suppress the independence of the others.

Dawkins went out to Panamá and made personal contact with all the delegates. He reported to Canning that peace with Spain was the first thing that all the deputies wanted. The purchase of recognition, he says, was not objected to in principle; but since it involved a responsibility beyond the powers which they brought to Panamá, they postponed the question to the next congress—which never took place. A military convention was concluded; but that was more in the hope of frightening King Ferdinand than for the purpose of aggression. Dawkins considered that there was power in the Congress to give security against any measure which Canning might think objectionable. By that, he meant that one country would be a check upon another. Colombia, he thought, would thwart the inclination of Mexico to invade Cuba or Puerto Rico; Mexico and Peru would oppose the unorthodox commercial principles attributed to Colombia, and would stand out against any undue influence on the part of the United States. "I found," he adds significantly, "the principles of all the deputies much less republican than I had expected. General Bolívar's favourable opinion of monarchy is evident." Republicanism still seemed to European diplomats to be synonymous with "revolutionary," and they could not understand how a man like Bolívar, if he were really a republican, could possibly be on the side of law and order.

Dawkins hardly realized how important the Congress was. Nor did the governments which kept away from it. Its real failure lay in the fact that it did not meet again, for Bolívar's ideas were more than a hundred years ahead of his time. The Congress might have established a league of American nations which included Britain; but Bolívar's league was weakened by the lack of British support, as the Geneva League a hundred years later was made ineffective by the isolationism of the United States. Again, for the first time in modern history, the principle of arbitration was introduced with plans for mediation and conciliation in cases of disagreement; and all secret treaties, agreements and subsidies, which might help to make war inevitable, were discouraged.

Unfortunately, neither the situation of those new republics, nor the general condition of South America at the time, was propitious for so far-reaching a plan of international settlement. First, Buenos Aires went to war with Brazil for the possession of the *Banda Oriental*, which afterwards, through the efforts of Britain, became the independent buffer-state, Uruguay. Salvador fell out with Guatemala, Mexico became a land of violent unrest, Chile spent its time in the discussion of rival constitutional theories. Bolivia, full of restless militarists, compelled the gentle

Sucre to leave the presidency, and ended by losing territory to all its neighbours, becoming an entirely inland country, deprived of all direct access to the sea. Peru made war on Colombia, which had freed it from Spain; Venezuela refused to acknowledge the Colombian Government any further, and seceded from the Union.

In 1815, in his letter from Jamaica, Bolívar had written:

> "It is a magnificent idea to try to form the whole of the New World into a single nation. . . . But it is impossible; for distinct climates, different geographical conditions, conflicting interests, opposing character, all combine to keep America divided."

His plan for a Pan-American Congress met with much opposition in America, and scarcely veiled hostility in Europe—hostility mingled with incredulity. He knew that it had great possibilities, and was bitterly disappointed at its failure. It was the first of the great disillusions which fell upon him in the last years of his life.

> "For many years," O'Leary relates, "the Liberator had hoped that the Congress of Panamá, if it could be arranged, would be of immense benefit to the new republics, confirming them in their independence, putting them in contact with one another, and binding them more closely together. It would create a spirit of unity and patriotism which would make them happy at home and respected abroad."

The achievement certainly fell far short of the intention, and Bolívar said bitterly that he was like the ancient Greek madman, who sat on a rock in the middle of the sea and tried to steer the ships sailing round him.

Chapter Ten

Disillusion

AFTER the victory of Ayacucho in 1824 and the triumphal progress to Potosí, Bolívar's fortunes declined. It is not enough to look for explanation in a physical or mental decline in the Liberator himself. He was prematurely aged, of course; but the arduous campaigns and the sudden changes of climate had done him less harm than indigestion or the air of Lima, the sweet cakes, and the perpetual adoration of incautious admirers, whose hymns to him were sung in the cathedral between the epistle and the gospel. Love-affairs have been alleged a cause of decline; but it is not proved that Bolívar was more amorous than many of his contemporaries. Women threw themselves at him, but he seems to have been no more sensual than the mean sensual man. To some he seemed less so; in London—the London of the Regent, of Rowlandson and Gilray—he had been mistaken for *algún griego pederasta.* Since the death of his wife he had never married again, and though never promiscuous like Miranda, after 1813 he was seldom without a *maîtresse en titre.*

The middle years were filled with the conscious

effort to make himself into a soldier and a leader of men: the only way to the one great ambition of his life—the liberation of his country from Spain. It is sometimes said that great soldiers are born, not made. Bolívar certainly was not born one. His early service in the militia was no more than a picnic in fine clothes; he first saw active service as A.D.C. to one of the aristocratic Creole commanders sent by Miranda—unsuccessfully—to check the Royalists in 1811. He set himself to learn the soldier's trade, from the beginning, and then the business of a commander; he read lives of Napoleon, accounts of his campaigns and elementary books on strategy. One of the main reasons for his success was that he always put the army first, and, above everything, the welfare of the private soldier; that was a side of the art of war which he learnt supremely well, as we can see from the way he was adored by his men. In the Llanos he led the same life as the troops, and wore the same uniform: flannel tunic, linen breeches, high boots and cloth forage cap. One day, when his cap fell into the river and was carried away by the current, the English cheered lustily—to bring good luck, it was thought. Among the officers he had his likes and his dislikes. There were some of his European officers, like Ducoudray-Holstein and Hippisley, who behaved badly and had to be sent home, where they wrote books attacking the Liberator and all that he stood for. Others had to be promoted to good jobs elsewhere. But there were others, again, like O'Leary, Belford Wilson and Ferguson, to whom he took a fancy; and they stayed with him faithfully, though they got less promotion for doing so and found the Liberator often irritable and always exacting. "His imperious and impatient temperament would never tolerate the smallest delay in the execution of an order," O'Leary says. "One had to be off at a gallop and comply with the order at once."

O'Leary describes Bolívar having dark hair, though it began to turn grey in 1821. He wore a moustache and whiskers, but shaved them off at Potosí, in 1825. He stood five feet six inches, had a narrow chest, a thin body, thin legs and small hands and feet. His skin had become dark and rather rough, through exposure on his campaigns in the tropics. Larrazábal describes his manner as lively and decided. He held his head high, his step was firm, his aspect frank and open, and his personal attraction irresistible. His forehead was high, his eyebrows thick and arched, his eyes large and wide-awake, his look "penetrating and electric," recalling in this the "dark and penetrating gaze" described by General Miller. His look was pleasant, O'Leary thought when he was in a good humour, but terrible in moments of irritation; the difference was most marked. He was careful in his dress, and had a bath every day; in hot climates, he sometimes had as many as three. He spoke quickly, in a rather high-pitched voice that was sometimes hoarse. He was extremely loyal to his friends, and would not allow you to speak ill of anyone in his presence. Friendship, *amistad,* was a word that was sacred with him. He was confiding as none other, but never forgave anyone who had abused his confidence. His personal generosity bordered on the prodigal; but he was very close, O'Leary noticed, with public funds. He dictated his letters swinging himself in his hammock, or pacing the room with folded arms; a characteristic attitude with him was to clutch the collar of his tunic with his left hand while the first finger of his right hand rested on his upper lip. He could dictate to three secretaries at a time, and never left a letter unanswered, however humble the writer.

Being himself a cultured man with the temperament of an intellectual as well as a romantic man of action, Bolívar annoyed the well-educated but anti-intellectual type. He could make himself at home with the learned and with the illiterate; but not with the deliberate low-brows, who found him difficult and often disliked him intensely, and their dislike has been inherited by some modern biographers. Again, his devotion to dashing and attractive young regimental officers, like the Colombian Girardot, knew no bounds, nor did his grief at the news of Girardot's death in action; all Venezuelans were ordered to wear mourning for a month, the hero's heart was carried in solemn procession to Caracas and laid in a monument specially erected in the Cathedral. Sucre was another example. Bolívar picked him out for personal reasons; he had military qualities of the highest order, and never let the Liberator down; those who had ever felt personal devotion to Bolívar never did. He was a shrewd judge of character, and could distinguish the man who would follow him from feelings of personal devotion from the other who merely obeyed orders and looked after his own interests. Another of his discoveries was the young Irish volunteer, Daniel O'Leary, the most devoted of his followers while he was alive and the one who, by his immense and impartial collection of letters and documents and by the *Life* founded on them, did more for Bolívar's memory than anyone else.[1]

There was a period when all Bolívar's ideas and interests were concentrated on the army: the details of organization and supply, personal qualities and personal affections. Gradually, however, he began to feel the need for feminine society also. From 1813 to 1819 his favourite was Josefina Machado. She went with him on some of his campaigns, and was known to the army as *La Señorita Pepa*. Another name which appears is that of Anita Lenoir. From 1822 his companion was Manuela Saenz, a great-hearted woman, worthy of the Liberator as he was of her.

[1] It is strange that O'Leary's *Memoirs* have never been printed in English, the language in which they were originally written.

She had been married to a Dr. Thorne, an Englishman; but she left him for Bolívar and refused all exhortations to return. Dr. Thorne was eccentric, uxorious and recklessly generous. He sent her large sums of money (which she refused) and left her all his fortune in his will. He was always begging her to come back to him; but Manuela always declined. She wrote spirited letters, as the following example will show.

"No, no, no! No more, man; for God's sake! Why do you force me to write and break my resolution? What do you gain by it, except the pain you give me by telling you *No* a thousand times? Oh, sir! you are excellent, you are inimitable. I will never say anything except how good you are. But, my friend, to leave you for General Bolívar is something; to leave any other husband without your good qualities would be nothing. And yet you think that I, after being the General's lover for seven years, and with the absolute certainty of having his whole heart, would prefer to be married to the Father, the Son, the Holy Ghost or the Holy Trinity! If I regret anything, it is that you were not even better than you are, so that I could have left you all the same. I know quite well that nothing can unite me to him under the auspices of what you call honour. Do you think me less honoured because he is my lover and not my husband? Oh, I don't live under the social preoccupations invented for people to torment one another! Leave me alone, my dear Englishman. We will do something else: In heaven we will be married again; but not on earth. Do you think this a bad arrangement? If you do, I can tell you that you are very difficult to please. In the heavenly country we will live an angelic and wholly spiritual life (for as a man you are a bore). There, everything will be as it is in England; for the monotonous life is reserved for your nation (in love-making, I mean; for in other things, who are cleverer at shipping or commerce?). You prefer love without pleasure, conversation without wit, walking slowly, greeting with reverence, getting up carefully and sitting down, joking without laughing. These are divine politenesses; but I, miserable mortal . . . I want to laugh at myself, at you and at all those serious English ways. How badly I should get on in heaven! As badly as if I went to live in England, or Constantinople; for the English give me the idea that they are tyrants with women, though you were not one with me, but certainly more jealous than a Portuguese. That is not what I want! Have I not good taste? But joking apart: politely and without a smile, with all the seriousness, truth and purity of an English lady, I tell you that *I will never come back to you!* You, Church of England, and I an atheist: that is the strongest religious impediment; and the fact that I am in love with someone else is a greater and stronger impediment still. Don't you see how formally correct my thoughts are?

"Your invariable friend,

" MANUELA."

She signed it with a long, curly continuation of the last A; but in her rough copy (for, like Bolívar, she kept rough copies of her letters) she added in the margin:

> "N.B. My husband is a Catholic, and I was never an atheist; only the longing to be separated from him made me write like this."

Actually, her letter-writing was one of the things about her that Bolívar found most attractive. In one of his earliest letters to her, he admires her literary style. She appears frequently in memoirs of the time. In Lima she rode astride a spirited horse, escorted by two Colombian lancers, and dressed in a scarlet tunic with gold facings and white riding breeches. "She was a strong woman," the writer adds; "she could control her nerves, and be calm and energetic when bullets were flying and swords stained with blood." In Bogotá she would appear on horseback in officer's uniform, followed by two negresses dressed as hussars; they were called Nathan and Jonathan. In this garb she rode out in a rage, on the eve of Corpus Christi 1830, to avenge an insult to the Liberator, a drawn sword in her hand and her two negresses armed with lances. She burst into the big square, the *Plaza Mayor*, scattered the crowd, rode over the policemen on duty, and broke up two large set-pieces of fireworks in which were said to be figures caricaturing Bolívar. She read books, too; liked Plutarch and Tacitus, and could recite long pieces from the Spanish classics. After the Colombian Union had split up into its original components, she retired to the little port of Paita in northern Peru: a hot climate, where most of the houses were open all round, to catch any breeze there might be. From there sixteen years afterwards, in 1846, she sent O'Leary a little box, full of intimate letters from Bolívar; but very few of them appear in the large volumes of his published correspondence.

One morning in 1851, a small British steamer put into Paita for twelve hours, and the passengers disembarked to stretch their legs. Among them was another Liberator, Garibaldi, who, after his defence of Rome in 1849, had made his way to New York and then to Panamá where he had been ill with malaria. The sea air had done him good, and he went ashore with the others. He was invited to the house of a generous and hospitable inhabitant of the place, a lady who had been in bed for some years with paralysis. He spent the greater part of the day at her bedside, lying on a sofa. The lady was Manuela Saenz, *La più graziosa e gentile matrona ch'io abbia mai veduta*, Garibaldi says; the most charming and gracious lady he had ever seen.

"Having been the friend of Bolívar, she knew the smallest details of the life of the great Liberator of America; but neither his life, entirely given up to the emancipation of his country, nor the highest qualities which adorned him, could suffice to preserve him from the poison of envy and jesuitry by which his last days were embittered. It is the old, old story: Socrates, Christ, Columbus; and the world always remains a prey to miserable nonentities who only know how to deceive! After that day which I shall always think of as delicious in comparison with so much suffering, because it was spent in the company of so interesting an invalid, I left her really moved."

The greatest moment of Manuela's life came on the night of the 25th September, 1828, when there was an attempt on Bolívar's life, in Bogotá.

It may seem surprising that the Liberator should have become so unpopular, even with a minority, but the causes were many. They were partly personal. Bolívar was a man only able to live at a high pitch; his great anticipations were followed by inevitable reactions, which made him moody, difficult and short-tempered: harsh to his friends and impossible to his enemies. In public life the seeds of unpopularity grew up around the form of government, the fact of dominions which had formerly been quite separate from one another under the Spanish Empire now being included in the Colombian Union. In Colombia, the objections were mainly political; in Venezuela, there were serious economic grounds for discontent. But though most Venezuelans wished to separate from Colombia, they were loyal on the whole to Bolívar because they believed that he would obtain separation for them. In each country of the Colombian Union, Bolívar's magnificent idea of a large, powerful, Spanish-speaking state broke before the deeply rooted Spanish sense of separatism. *La patria chica*, the little country; my own little country, right or wrong! It was the old Iberian feeling for local independence, which no ruler of Spanish peoples, since the time of the Romans, has ever solved successfully or solved for long.

In South America, Bolívar's ideas seemed too eighteenth century and too French—at least for the politically minded part of the population; and while the Liberator saw only too clearly that, with a backward and largely illiterate people, there was no safe and practical system which was not strongly centralized, his political enemies were always working for federalism and separatism. Federalism, in Bolívar's view, meant an international federation of strongly centralized republics: Venezuela, Colombia, Ecuador, Peru and Bolivia. For his political opponents, it meant a system of federal provinces within each independent republic. This worked well enough in North America, with a population accustomed for centuries to local self-management in their political and ecclesiastical affairs; but it was hopeless in the thinly populated semi-tropical countries of the South, inhabited by various races of men who had hardly ever had a say in their civil administration, and never a word in their ecclesiastical government. By European diplomats, this lack of political experience in South American states was usually ascribed to their republican form of government. The wonder is that they were able to make a republican system work at all. They had had no experience of any form of government except absolute monarchy; and even when the political bonds with Spain had snapped, the bonds of ecclesiastical union and sympathy remained, in the power and influence of the Roman Catholic Church.

In Bolívar's last years resentment came not only from conservatives but also from liberals. They disapproved of the excessive centralization of the Colombian Government, and the autocratic actions which that government found necessary. In other countries of the Union, too, many people resented Colombian hegemony; why should they all be governed from Bogotá? The separatist movement was most active in Venezuela, where it had got hold of General Páez, a man who was inclined to see everything from the point of view of the *patria chica*, which in his case meant the wide river plains of the Orinoco. The City Council of Caracas also was opposed to the dictation of Bogotá. In some decrees of the central government the municipal authorities thought they detected violations of the Constitution; and this spirit of independence, which was imitated by other municipalities as well, shows how the tradition of the old Spanish municipal councils had survived in the new South American Republics. They were always on their guard against any attempt to usurp their powers, and were as much an obstacle to Bolívar's centralized government as three centuries before in Spain they had been to the unified administration of Ferdinand and Isabel. In America, they were not democratic and had been declining rapidly under the Republican Government; in some places even they had disappeared when the federal system was introduced into the Constitution.

In Venezuela the climax came over the question of calling up recruits. Páez at first let things slide; then his troops carried out the decree of conscription with the careless brutality of a press-gang. The effect on the population was to turn them, not against Páez, but against the central government at Bogotá, so that eventually they were ready to follow Páez into secession from the Colombian Union. Bolívar sent O'Leary, at that time his first A.D.C., to see if an amicable settlement could be reached. The journey from Lima to Valencia took him nine weeks, and when he arrived, Páez had already gone south to his *patria chica* on the upper branches of the Orinoco. O'Leary found him at Achaguas on 19th August, 1828, sitting on a low stool with a violin in his hands, listening to a blind Indian singing on a chair in front of him. Páez was sensitive to music. He did not like music to be interrupted. O'Leary made a bad impression.

He spent a fortnight in trying to win over the astute cowboy general. Páez was cleverer than he thought. He had a way of keeping quiet when better-educated people were talking, but he was a shrewd judge of men and could see which way the wind was blowing. On this occasion, he gave all the stock, slick answers of a typical rebel general—the type well known in Spain and the Spanish-speaking countries from that day to this. He had no other object, he said, than to save his country from anarchy. It was essential that he should continue in his command; and though no one regretted what had happened more than he did, it was no longer in his power to remedy it. O'Leary saw at last that he could do nothing, and returned to Bolívar to report. He had a bad reception. Bolívar did not understand why he had taken so long, and then could only report failure; he suspected that O'Leary had become an instrument of the tortuous policy of General Santander, the Vice-President. It was quite untrue; O'Leary was unfailingly loyal to Bolívar; but he had misjudged the intelligence of Páez and did not know how to approach him—a man of no education, more interested in learning old tunes from a blind Indian than in receiving an emissary from the Liberator of America.

Bolívar set out on the long journey to Venezuela, from Peru and Bogotá, preceded by his English A.D.C., Colonel Ferguson. One of the first things he read on crossing the Venezuelan border was a proclamation by Páez in favour of secession. He wrote him a letter of friendly reproach. Bolívar was determined not to allow the issue of secession to lead to civil war. On 10th January, 1827, he rode into Caracas accompanied by Páez.

Bolívar at once set to work to improve all branches of the administration. During his absence, everything had fallen into neglect. There seemed to be hardly a single law of the Republic of Great Colombia which was obeyed in Venezuela; the secessionists were not far wrong when they said that union had led them backward rather than forward. The University of Caracas and the Schools were in a precarious state; the stipends of teachers were paid, if at all, at irregular intervals; and the funds which Great Colombia could afford for education were mainly spent in Bogotá. Bolívar did his best to set aside special funds for education in Venezuela, and made proposals for its thorough reorganization. Again, the money set aside for the freeing of slaves was not, he found, being used for its real object. About two-thirds of it seemed to be spent for other purposes.

The most serious feature in the condition of Venezuela was the decline in agriculture and cattle-raising. The prosperity of the end of the colonial period had gone. The tobacco crop had shrunk to a small fraction of what it had been, and was all bought up at the lowest price by a foreign firm. Coffee was in much the same case. "The principal failure of our agriculture," it was reported in 1828, "is due to the destitution of the owners of the plantations. To get in his crop or clean his land, the owner has to borrow money at a ruinous rate of interest, sometimes as much as 15 per cent. per mensem. The consequence is that all profit goes to the money-lender, and the country is being ruined because no one can afford to plant a single tree." Then there was the enormous wastage of cattle and horses, by both royalists and patriots, during the wars of independence. Owners of plantations not more than 70 or 80 miles from the capital had to hand over something like half their total crop to the waggoners who took it to market; they seemed to have no transport of their own, and some had given up and gone away, leaving their plantations to run wild and go out of cultivation.

For six months Bolívar strove to put some order into agriculture, finance, the law-courts and every branch of the government of the country. On 4th July, 1828, he set out for Bogotá, leaving Páez in charge. He never returned to Caracas.

Bolívar was blamed, even by some of his friends, for yielding to the Venezuelan separatists and confirming Páez in his command. He had sacrificed, they said, both the majesty of the law and the authority of Congress. But what else could he have done? The Revolution had already taken place. It had obtained local autonomy which, in less than three years, was to be converted into a new, independent, federal republic, known to-day as the United States of Venezuela. Bolívar might possibly have remained in Venezuela and tried to put the constitutional machine together again; but by doing so he would have lost all authority over the rest of the Colombian Union. The other alternative was to go back through Bogotá and try to put a stop to insurrection in the South. Bolívar chose the second alternative, and his choice once more showed his political wisdom.

For reasons not unlike those which had determined the course of events in Venezuela, the departments of Quito and Guayaquil were against the Constitution of Great Colombia. Only the personal influence of Bolívar and the prestige of his name could hold them in the Colombian Union. During the year 1826 both Quito and Guayaquil declared, through their municipal councils, that they resumed full sovereignty over their own territories, while placing themselves unreservedly in the hands of Bolívar. He managed for a time to check these separatist movements; but as soon as his back was turned, both departments fell into a state of permanent anarchy.

Dictatorship and anarchy, a Venezuelan historian has remarked, are the terms which best describe the condition of the Colombian Union after 1826: dictatorship when Bolívar was there, anarchy when he was away. Dictatorship had been thrust upon him, and Peru had perhaps shown him that it was a system which worked. At least, it worked for a time, in a newly emancipated Spanish colony when the dictator was Bolívar. But in the long run it failed, and it set a shocking example to his successors throughout the nineteenth century.

Even while he was at Caracas, Bolívar had heard that down at Lima, hundreds of miles away, units of the Colombian army of liberation had revolted. The immediate result was that the inhabitants of Lima revolted too. They demanded the resignation of the government, and a federal constitution instead of the existing centralist regime. When Bolívar reached Bogotá from Caracas, on his way to Lima, he found that the opposition had become a strong, active party, inspired and led by Vice-President Santander. It called itself "Liberal" and stigmatized the followers of Bolívar as "Goths"—the common technique, only too familiar since, by which a reactionary party claims the credit for being more progressive than its opponents. Bolívar gave up the idea of going on to Lima. The Colombian Congress had decided, before his return, to convoke a Grand Convention at Ocaña, in March 1828, to examine the basis of the constitution, and perhaps reform it. In the ordinary course of events, the existing constitution would have had to run for not less than ten years before it could be amended; and the decision of Congress to amend it at that time was illegal. The situation seemed to Bolívar so precarious, that, as President of the Colombian Union, he felt obliged once more to decree himself the special powers allowed by the constitution in times of emergency. He ordered trial by court martial for all acts of conspiracy likely to prejudice public order; and to get rid of Vice-President Santander—for the moment, at any rate—he disposed that the government should be in the hands of the principal secretaries of state: the permanent officials, heads of their respective departments. He had little hope, now, for the survival of the Great Colombian Union.

When the Convention assembled at Ocaña, two parties appeared with aims and policies which were incompatible. One was centralist and in favour of the personal rule of Bolívar; the other was federalist and willing to further the ambition of Santander. From the first, it was clear that agreement was impossible, and compromise a thing that was unknown. Reading the debates in the Congress at Bogotá or the Convention at Ocaña, one becomes aware that the speakers are very like the members of the committees, boards and councils in which every inhabitant of a modern democratic country has to take part. The passions and the motives are the same: with some, nobility of mind, intellectual integrity, devotion to an ideal or a man; with others, petty jealousies, meaner motives, bargaining, *Kuhhandel*, and the incapacity to see that anyone can be acting from higher motives or a greater breadth of vision than their own. The chief failing in South America—and it was sometimes startling in its results—was inexperience: inexperience in the debaters and still more in the chairmen; the consciousness of the speakers that they were playing with a new toy or machine—government by discussion—which no one in South America before their generation had been able to touch; and then there was the uncertainty as to what the powers and duties of a chairman really were or how they could best be used for the public good. If the debaters talked at inordinate length, and did not shrink from the most violent personal abuse, the chairman was apt to become a nonentity who could only perform his functions with the consent of those present, or else a dictator whose word alone was law. Parliamentary methods need the sheltering, guiding tradition of centuries of self-government by discussion; whereas the newly independent Spanish-speaking republics of South America had been reared on three centuries of absolute monarchy.

Bolívar's presidential message to the Convention was a criticism of the Colombian Constitution of 1821, the constitution of Cúcuta. He had never really agreed with it; it did not represent his own views, as the constitutions of Angostura and Bolivia had done. In his opinion—and it would also have been the opinion of Montesquieu, to whom Bolívar owed so much of his political thought—those who framed the Colombian Constitution of 1821 "had fallen into the capital error of making the legislative power the sole sovereign body in the State." Instead of making the President equal in power to Congress, they had weakened him to such an extent that he had never been able either "to repel a foreign invasion or restrain an outbreak of sedition, unless armed with dictatorial powers."

So far Bolívar had reason on his side; but then he attacked the municipal councils—the only political tradition which they could really call their own. It was perhaps the first sign of that hardening of the arteries of his mind which set in rapidly during the last years of his life; a bitterness which drove him not only to dictatorship but to reaction. Yet he was not altogether wrong in his attitude to the council. The municipalities, he said, would be useful advisory bodies for provincial governors; but they had hardly ever fulfilled their true functions. Some had turned into debating societies, others had encouraged sedition, or merely made themselves unpopular through the taxes they levied. No decree would be more popular than one by which the municipal councils were abolished. He ended by an appeal for laws that were "inexorable" and were applied impartially to all. He could hardly help thinking how far away the present state of affairs had drifted from the ideal Republic which he had imagined in Angostura and Bolivia: a compromise between the English monarchy and the republic of the United States.

All this was infuriating to the supporters of Vice-President Santander. What he thought of the President is shown in a letter, intercepted by an officer who was loyal to Bolívar, but addressed to the Colombian chargé d'affaires in Washington. "Our country," Santander said, "is ruled by Bolívar, not constitutionally, but capriciously; with the purely honorary title of Liberator he has tried to give himself a title of authority above the law. . . . Do you imagine that any man of honour can be reconciled to this supreme disturber of the Republic? It is impossible to be reconciled to a chief who treats us as rebels and traitors . . . and makes no appointment to public office nor to his councils except to sworn friends of eternal dictatorship or the Bolivian Constitution . . . I am not going to be imprudent or immoderate at the Convention; I shall only consider the interests of the country by checking the colossal power of Bolívar, assure the rights of the people and those of the citizens, and divide the executive so as to contain it. You understand what I mean by this last phrase? I mean that I am for federalism, the only means left to us of saving the liberties of the nation."

The federalism of the United States was limited and centripetal, whereas the conception of federalism among Bolívar's opponents was centrifugal and tended towards complete separation. Bolívar aimed at a large, centralized Great Colombia, formed by independent countries coming together, as had happened with Switzerland, the Netherlands and the United States. Santander wanted the old Spanish provinces to remain independent, but with an additional federal system set up in the interior of each of them. It may be questionable which solution was right; but there can be no question that Santander had made a clever political move.

The friends of Bolívar saw through it at once: Vice-President Santander was only thinking of stepping into the Liberator's shoes. There was nothing to show that he would pay more respect to the law than Bolívar had; and it was a choice between one autocrat and another. Bolívar was certainly to be preferred, for after all, it was to him that the Republic owed its existence.

Chapter Eleven

Rejection

WHILE the Congress was sitting, Bolívar stayed not far off at Bucaramanga, near the Venezuelan border; and it was there, at one of the most disillusioned moments of his life, that a French officer attached to his staff recorded his table-talk. When all the circumstances are considered, we may wonder that the record is not more bitter than it is, for Lacroix's *Diario de Bucaramanga* gives so lifelike a portrait of the Liberator that a modern reader can almost hear him and see him: listening to the reports read by a secretary, dictating letters and whistling a French revolutionary song while the secretary finished the sentence, telling stories at dinner about Europe—and particularly about Paris; riding about the country and being polite to an old woman who thought him not smart enough for a general, let alone for the Liberator; going to church, not quite sure when to stand up or when to kneel down, but reprimanding his English doctor for sitting with crossed legs.

He was at a loose end at Bucaramanga. One day he would say that he was going down to Cartagena, to settle a difference between two

Colombian generals, each of whom thought he was commander of the port. Another day he would declare that if only the Convention would nominate his successor he would retire to Venezuela or go and live in Europe. So few people would believe that he had no personal ambitions! He would go away, to prove that they were wrong; and if at any time the existence of Colombia depended on his return, he would let it perish, rather than take command again. A week later, he was even more decided; "I will go! And 5,000 or 10,000 miles away I shall hear the din of civil war. But I shall not come back, you may be sure! . . . to a country which has driven me out with such indignity!" His spirits rose when he heard that the Convention had rejected the federal project; but a few days later he thought that federalism would come after all, and in that case it would be better—and avoid the danger of civil war—to aim at dividing the Colombian Union into three or four separate republics, united in a confederation for common defence.

He felt ill and discouraged. He changed his mind frequently, according to the views of the last person he had seen. His friends grew alarmed and gave him bad advice. "To leave the field to the enemy is to admit defeat!" they told him. "People will never say that you resigned your command because you thought it the best thing you could do. They will think you lost it because you could not keep it, or had personal ambitions which you could not achieve. San Martín resigned his command, and no one has ever forgiven him for it." Others thought that he should go on governing as dictator. "You will have the people's votes; and you ought not to mind, for the moment, being called a usurper. You alone can put Colombia on the right road. You cannot allow all your work to be undone." They sent O'Leary to Bucaramanga, one of the few men, besides his English aides, Wilson and Ferguson, who was believed to have the Liberator's complete confidence. Bolívar hesitated again. In the end the "Bolivianos" at the Convention were outvoted; and after a few more proposals and amendments, they left the town. The Convention of Ocaña broke up, leaving everything unsettled.

The first result was that the municipalities of Colombia refused to accept any decision which had been taken at Ocaña. In Bogotá, a *cabildo abierto*, an open council like those of twenty years before, decided not to be influenced by the Convention, but to give all power to Bolívar. Other municipalities did the same. They called for Bolívar, and demanded that he should be vested with supreme authority until it should be convenient for elections to be held. In Venezuela the municipal councils issued pronouncements in the same sense. Páez was indifferent, so long as he was left in command in his own part of the country. Bolívar could only accept the inevitable—the part of dictator—and play it to the best of his ability. To the general surprise he began to play it in a spirit that was reactionary, and even clerical.

Bolívar had never had any great illusions on the possibility of applying democratic principles whole-heartedly in South America; and some of his biographers have considered that, once in supreme command, he took little trouble to conceal his impatience with doubting liberals. The first thing was to restore order; and he did not hesitate to sacrifice personal liberties in order to do so. To stamp out anarchy, he employed all the forces of reaction; and the chief forces which could serve his purpose, in a country where all political tradition had been lost in the wars of independence, were just those forces which were most damaging to his political ideals: the army and the church. The army was represented by ambitious generals who were hoping to carve provinces for themselves out of the remains of the Colombian Union; there was not one of sufficient stature to dream of succeeding Bolívar. Sucre might have done so, but he was murdered not long before Bolívar's own death. There remained the clergy, supported by the religiosity of the rich and the fanaticism of the poor; and these, Bolívar resolved to exploit. His decrees show him bent on suppressing liberalism, which all dictators have invariably regarded as the fountain-head of anarchy; and he increased the army to something like four times its original size. With the church on his side, and the army—and his own personal influence, which was still considerable—Bolívar thought that the Colombian Union might still be saved.

Bolívar's dictatorship was at once acknowledged by Páez. The astute *llanero* saw that the independence of Venezuela was now assured; it was already a state within a state, and he meant to keep a free hand in the country which he already ruled. Bolívar realized this; yet he was always conciliatory, and his letters to Páez are written in the friendliest terms.

In Colombia, Bolívar's enemies took to conspiracy, though Páez would not let them cross the border and conspire on Venezuelan soil. "Behead Bolívar," one of their wits remarked, "cut off his feet, and you are left with *oliva*, the symbol of peace and tranquillity." Their aim, as one of the survivors described it, 25 years afterwards, was to capture Bolívar and his ministers and put Santander at the head of the government. Santander was certainly privy to the plot. There was talk of assassination; but an attempt on Bolívar, when riding with two friends near Bogotá, was frustrated by Santander himself. That was on the 21st September; the next attempt was fixed for the 28th. But on the 25th one of the conspirators was arrested, and the others determined to act that same night before he could give anything away under cross-examination.

Bolívar had been warned, but he thought that the usual guard at the Presidential Palace—the old Palacio de San Carlos—was enough. O'Leary was away; all the other aides, except one, were on sick leave. The Liberator, too, was feeling ill and depressed. The faithful who saw eye to eye with him were few. His presence still aroused enthusiasm and devotion, but he could not himself be everywhere at once. Even his presence was not so effective as it used to be. Formerly he had only to appear in person, and the waverers became loyal again; a few days or weeks of office-work and personal rounds of inspection had always put things to rights. Now, however, there were intrigues against him personally. That, perhaps, was natural with a dictator; and in Peru, too, they had insisted on his assuming dictatorial powers. The stigma of dictatorship never left him, and his personal intervention in any question was branded by his enemies as dictatorial. The plot in Bogotá was against his dictatorial power. Though the organizers were middle-aged intriguers and wire-pullers, the actual executants were mainly young men, with the fanatical faith of storm-troopers, relying on methods of terrorism. "We could not flatter ourselves with the thought of success, except by the impression of terror which the news of Bolívar's death would produce on our opponents."

One of the assassins is speaking. Vice-President Santander, without being directly implicated himself, seems to have known that a new attempt was to be made; yet he gave Bolívar no warning, and did nothing to check the movement. He too had been intriguing against the Liberator, as intercepted letters showed. Bolívar had good reason to be discouraged.

On the night of the attempt the conspirators hid in the cathedral till midnight. It had been raining—the climate of Bogotá has been compared to a cold spring in Paris—but there was bright moonlight. One brigade of artillery had been won over by the conspirators; each knew exactly what he had to do, and they felt confident of success. The clock struck 12. They came out of the cathedral and got to work.

In his depression, and the rain, and the chilly afternoon, Bolívar had sent for Manuela Saenz. She grumbled at having to go out just then, but duly came to the Palace. Bolívar was having a hot bath. She read to him while he lay in it, and then put him to bed. He seemed to have a feverish cold, and she stayed with him.

Manuela described what happened next:

> "It was about 12 when the Liberator's dogs began to bark; and there was a peculiar noise which must have been the fight with the sentries, but no shooting. I woke the Liberator, and the first thing he did was to pick up a sword and a pistol and try to open the door.

I stopped him and made him dress, which he did quite calmly but quickly. He said: 'Bravo! Well, here I am dressed; what do we do now? Barricade ourselves in?' He tried to open the door again, but I prevented him. Then I remembered something I had once heard the General say. 'Didn't you tell Pepe Paris,' I said, 'that that window would do for an occasion like this?' 'You're right,' he answered and went over to the window. I prevented him getting out at first, because there were people passing; but he managed it when they had gone, just as the door was being broken open [in the next room]. I went to meet them, to give him time to get away; but I didn't have time to see him jump, or to shut the window. As soon as they saw me, they seized me and said: 'Where's Bolívar?' I told them he was at a meeting, which was the first thing that occurred to me. They searched the outer room carefully and went on to the second, and when they saw the window open, they exclaimed: 'He's got away! He's escaped.' I said: 'No, *señores*, he has not got away: he's at a meeting' . . . I said I knew there was a meeting, and that the Liberator went to it every night, but I didn't know where it was. At this they grew very angry, and dragged me away with them until we found Ibarra [an A.D.C.] lying wounded on the floor. 'So they've killed the Liberator?' he asked. 'No, Ibarra,' I said, 'the Liberator's alive.' I know it was stupid of us to talk, and I began to bandage him with a handkerchief. They asked me more questions; but as they couldn't get anything more they took me back to the room where they found me, and I brought the wounded man along too.

"Suddenly I heard the sound of heavy boots. I looked out of the window and saw Colonel Ferguson, running along from the house where he had been in bed with a sore throat. He saw me in the moonlight, which was bright just then. He asked for the Liberator, but I said I didn't know; and I couldn't tell him because of the guards they had left there, but I warned him not to come in because they would kill him. He answered that he would die doing his duty. In a moment I heard a shot . . . and then the blow on the head with a sabre which left him dead. . . .

"The Liberator had taken a pistol, and a sword which someone or other had given him in Europe. When he jumped into the street, his cook happened to be passing and went along with him. The General stood in the river [under a bridge] for some time; and then sent the man to see what was happening at the barracks. . . . I went as far as the cathedral, and there I saw the Liberator on a horse, talking to Santander and Padilla, with a crowd of soldiers cheering."

The rising was over in a few hours. By 4 a.m. Bolívar was back in the Presidential Palace. The conspiracy was crushed, but he had caught a chill from which he never recovered. It went to his lungs, and the effects of this attack of pleurisy never left him. The conspirators were rounded up, except for two or three who lived to conspire another day: one to write an impenitent account of the affair many years afterwards in Europe, and another to return and even become President of the Republic. Bolívar's first thought was to pardon them all; but the decision did not rest with him, and the faithful General Urdaneta had them dealt with summarily. Fourteen were shot. Santander was condemned to death, as accessory; but the sentence was commuted to one of banishment and loss of military rank, though he, too, eventually returned to be President of the Republic.

Bolívar was overwhelmed mentally and physically. He never recovered from the shock, and the tuberculosis made rapid strides. His letters, more voluble than ever, are sometimes incoherent, and his postscripts illegible.

> "I am so worried," he wrote on November 15th, 1828, "that I shall go away to the country for several months, to a place where there are nothing but Indians. . . . I can't put up any longer with such ingratitude. I'm not a saint, I've no wish to suffer martyrdom. Only the luck of having a few good friends keeps me going in this torture."

The dictatorship continued, either under Bolívar personally, or exercised by others in his name. Reaction was energetically pursued, centralism accentuated. "The Liberator," a Venezuelan historian has remarked, "in spite of his understanding of the French Revolution, and his knowledge of British constitutional practice, had become a doctrinaire administrator of the Latin type. He thought in 1828 as if he were living in ancient Rome—the ancient Rome of the eighteenth-century *philosophes*. He still believed in political 'virtue' and held that dictatorship was a sovereign remedy in times of emergency; but in this way he fell into what seem to us now the greatest errors of his public life." He did not pretend that dictatorship could be a permanent system of government; "his good intentions are as evident as the error in his calculations." His reliance on the army and the church, and his persecution of liberalism, have already been referred to. Like most dictators since his time, he found himself obliged to interfere with the text-books read in schools and colleges. The books to which his attention was specially drawn were written by an Englishman—Bentham—who had personally sent Bolívar some of his writings, translated into Spanish by a liberal Catalan exile in London. They were removed from the list of works prescribed for study, although afterwards they were reinstated, and held their place for nearly a hundred years.

Other repressive measures against liberalism followed, and by 1829 very few of the liberal principles remained which had inspired the declaration of Venezuelan independence—indeed, throughout the length and breadth of Great Colombia the only revolutionary idea which was still intact was the firm resolve never to return to the domination of Spain.

At the end of 1828 Bolívar suspended all the municipal councils. In Venezuela, many people approved, forgetting that the municipal councils had been, on the whole, the only organized bodies of resistance to arbitrary government, and the only effective centres of independence. They were not, of course, democratic; they represented oligarchy and the old Creole families, as we have seen. It was on them that Páez had founded his military authority. Yet in obedience to Bolívar he dissolved them forthwith, and handed over local government to *corregidores*, regional commissioners sent down from the capital.

The Colombian Union continued to exist in a precarious state: Venezuela practically independent under Páez, Quito in a state of perpetual anarchy; and now Peru, which had once begged for a Colombian army to deliver it from the Spaniards, made war on the country which had set it free. "Neither in Colombia nor in Peru can one get anything done," Bolívar exclaimed. "Not even my own name counts for anything now. Everything has gone, for good. . . . Instinct alone makes one go on living, but [life is] almost without an object."

There was a rising in the south of Colombia, at Popayán, and almost at the same time Quito was invaded by troops from Peru. Something of the Liberator's old activity returned. With the help of the Quito general, Flores, and the Colombian General Córdoba, he succeeded in rapidly suppressing the insurgents at Popayán; while Sucre, after a campaign "rendered particularly arduous by the extraordinary and unexpected strategical mistakes of the Peruvian commander," gained at Tarqui a crushing victory over a force twice the size of his own. Bolívar's troubles were not yet over, for his own General Córdoba rebelled in the autumn, against "the tyranny of Bolívar," and had to be routed at El Santuario by a force commanded by the faithful O'Leary.

Meanwhile the question of finding a successor to Bolívar was becoming urgent. In 1829 efforts were made to discover another man capable of holding the office of president-for-life. To the mind of the Liberator there was considerable difference between a president-for-life and a king or an emperor; but less subtle minds were unable to see this, and the idea had grown up that the life-presidency could be preserved by bringing in an English prince. The plan of a *monarquía inglesa,* a limited monarchy in the English style, has been attributed to Bolívar himself; it reappeared in 1829 and did considerable harm to his popularity. That Bolívar ever really wanted a crowned king or emperor in South America is extremely doubtful; those who attributed the idea to him were probably misled by wishful thinking, and the idea that he ever wanted a crown for himself is absurd to anyone acquainted with his character or political thought. The tragical history of the Emperor Itúrbide in Mexico showed what was likely to happen to successful Latin American generals when they aspired to the Imperial purple; and if a king were to be thought of for Great Colombia, it was essential that he should belong to one of the old royal families of Europe. The chief difficulty was that every department of Great Colombia was full of ambitious generals, or *caudillos*, ready to rise in their own immediate districts. It was plain that the Colombian Union could not continue to exist under republican institutions which demanded a presidential election every four years; and for that reason, and also because a life-presidency seemed too much like a dictatorship, opinion veered round to constitutional monarchy, for the order and stability which were believed to be inseparable from it. The Council of State in Bogotá tried to hold out to England and France the prospect of a monarchy after the Liberator's death; but Bolívar was thinking rather of some kind of mediation, influence, alliance or protectorate, by one of the great powers. He made declarations which were ambiguous and contradictory. He wrote from Quito in 1829, asking the Foreign Minister to sound the diplomatic representatives of Britain and the United States, adding that it would be impossible to prevent the outbreak of anarchy in Colombia, if some powerful state did not intervene. The choice seemed to be either anarchy or a return to something like colonial status.

> "There has been a Panamá congress of American nations, but it has been despised by the nations most interested. A federation has been proposed, between the three Sovereign States of Venezuela, Colombia and Quito; but there has been such misrepresentation and such an outcry, that it could have been heard in heaven. Britain has offered to mediate between Brazil and the River Plate; it has intervened by force of arms between Turkey and Greece. Could not something also be done about Colombia?"

Nothing was done; and the monarchical project was given up.

In 1830 the Colombian Union fell to pieces. First Venezuela assumed its independence, and then Quito; Bolívar's great dream was shattered.

From May 1830 until his death in December, Bolívar's life was a continual torment. He could not even do the last thing he had set his heart on doing: get away from Colombia altogether. His friends kept insisting that he should wait and see whether, at the last minute, something could not be done to preserve the Colombian Union; though by this time the Liberator knew that all further effort was vain and useless. The increasing hold which his illness had gained upon him condemned him to inaction; and nothing that even the most elementary medical science could do could help a man who refused to submit to almost any medical treatment whatever.

Above all, he was short of money, and could not think of beginning a long voyage until funds reached him from Caracas. This was exasperating to a man who had never had to think about money-matters and was of an extremely nervous temperament. He had once been a rich man; but his plantations had been fought over and destroyed, his houses were mostly in ruins, and his fortune had been reduced to his royalties on the copper mines at Aroa—royalties which for a long time had not been paid and were at that moment the subject of litigation. His lawyers did what they could to find him ready money; but they were unable to overcome the scarcely veiled hostility of Páez, now head of the independent Venezuelan Government, or the personal spite of a Dr. Yañes, the most influential lawyer in the country. Bolívar felt the indignity of it, and more, the base ingratitude. On his resignation from the presidency of the Colombian Union, Congress had confirmed a decree of 1823 granting him an annual pension of 30,000 pesos (say £6,000); but he had never received it, nor had he accepted the pension voted him by the Congress of Peru. It was impossible for a man like the Liberator to resign himself to economies, accustomed as he was to give away all the money he had by him, in charity or presents to old friends or old soldiers. One or two old friends, of the few he still had in Venezuela, tried to help him. His musical uncle, Estéban Palacios, who long ago had played string quartets in the garden at Chacao, offered him 5,000 pesos down, and 5,000 more which were invested in Europe. Bolívar felt he could not take them and declined.

At the end of September 1830, he moved along the coast to Soledad and Barranquilla. On 1st December he reached Santa Marta, a place where the hot wind blew sand in at every door and window—quite unsuitable for a man dying of consumption. "He came ashore in a carrying chair," his French doctor reported. "He was unable to walk. He was thin and emaciated in body and restless in mind. His voice was hoarse, he coughed perpetually, and the first diagnosis was that there were extensive pulmonary lesions." Next day the French doctor saw him in consultation with an American surgeon; they diagnosed pulmonary tuberculosis. On 6th December he was moved out into the country, to the Quinta de San Pedro Alejandrino, an estate belonging to a Spaniard, Joaquín de Mier. Spain was the country above all others which had cause to hate Bolívar; without him, and his twenty years' struggle, first for freedom and then for their existence as free states, Venezuela, Colombia,

Ecuador, Peru and Bolivia would still have been parts of the Spanish Empire. Yet now, when Venezuela and Colombia had turned their backs on him, Peru had forgotten him and Bolivia had set aside the constitution he had given it, it was a Spaniard who took him in, and housed him during his last illness. That action was a very Spanish thing.

In his last weeks Bolívar turned to Spanish books, particularly to *Don Quixote*, finding there, perhaps, his own image, as it was afterwards found by Unamuno.

"The three greatest *idiots* in history," he said in his bitterness, "have been Jesus Christ, Don Quixote and . . . myself!" The saying would have pleased Dostoievsky.

He had visits from a few old friends and comrades in arms; conversations with the doctor.

"Doctor, what did you come to this country to find?"

" Liberty."

" Have you found it?"

"Yes, General."

"Then you are more fortunate than I am. . . . Go back to your fair France, where the tricolour is still flying. Here, in this country, no one can live. Too many crooks; *canallas*."

At night he was delirious. He thought he was back among his own men. The watchers heard him say: "Come on now! Come on! *Vámonos!* . . . These people don't love us in this country . . .

Come on, boys! This way . . ." And then: "They may take my kit aboard now."

The Bishop of Santa Marta came, and told him it was time to do his duty as a Christian. Bolívar protested; he was tired, but not so ill as all that. Then he resigned himself to it, groaning: "Oh, how shall I get out of this labyrinth!" He confessed to the parish priest of an Indian village. It is doubtful whether he could be called a Catholic; a deist rather. He belonged to the Age of Reason; yet he had lived on into times when all that was, was unreason. Romantic. He himself would one day be considered one of the living spirits of the Romantic Movement. "All a jest, all dust, all nothing." All had not been a jest, certainly; but all was dust—it was blowing into the room through every crack and cranny—and all would soon be nothing. Rather than a Catholic or a deist, he was a *philosophe*, steeped in the thought of the French eighteenth century. Contrary to Catholic truth, he had always defended liberty of conscience and freedom for all forms of worship—except in that last exasperated period of dictatorship. Religion should be the law of the individual conscience; in the ideal constitutions which he had framed, no one religion was recognized as the established religion of the State. Yet as a public man, head of the government, he had felt bound to respect the forms and outward manifestations of Catholicism, which was the religion of the great majority of his fellow-countrymen and treat the Catholic Church as an important factor in political and social life, as it was among all people of Spanish origin.

On 10th December he made his will. He declared that he had no other property beyond the estate and mines of Aroa, and a few jewels in a safe at Cartagena. He left a gold medal to the Bolivian Congress, which had conferred it; and to the University Library at Caracas the copies of the *Contrat Social* of Rousseau and a book on military tactics which had once belonged to Napoleon, and had been given him by the father of his English A.D.C., Belford Wilson. His manservant was to receive 8,000 pesos, for long and faithful service; his residuary legatees were his sisters and his nephews. His executors were to convey a message of thanks to General Sir Robert Wilson, for the fine behaviour of his son, Colonel Belford Wilson. (Manuela Saenz was up at Bogotá, holding the position for the Liberator to the last.) After the will had been signed and witnessed, Bolívar dictated his last proclamation, "Colombians," he ended, "my latest wish is for the happiness of our country. If my death can help to put an end to party strife and consolidate the Union, I shall go down to the grave in peace."

He died a week later, on 17th December, 1830. O'Leary was there, Belford Wilson, and Andrés Ibarra who had lost an arm on the night of the mutiny at Bogotá. According to the Liberator's last instructions, such papers as he had by him were burnt; but the doctor declared that he had seen among them a petition to Bolívar to allow himself to be crowned. In the margin was scribbled in pencil:

> "To accept a crown would stain my reputation. I prefer the glorious title of First Citizen of Colombia."

Bolívar's life ended in defeat and disappointment. Had he lived in vain? His last proclamation went unheeded; he himself had been driven to repudiate his own political faith; his legacy was buried with him. But a hundred years afterwards, strange things began to happen on that continent where everything is strange and few things impossible. States began to settle their differences by arbitration, instead of war. Contrary to all expectation a stable republicanism was developed. In some countries (particularly Colombia and Uruguay) real liberalism was achieved; while between most of them a genuine, good-neighbourly feeling began to make its appearance.

Bolívar's work ended in ruins: but his ideal is still there, and the achievement of the Spanish and Portuguese Americas is one of the great facts of modern history. They are among the few peoples in the world to-day whose belief in the future has not been shaken, and whose ideals—

however Utopian they may have appeared in the time of the Liberator—are now plans which can and may be put into practice, even though they may not take the form of the close political union intended by Bolívar himself.

Appendix

NOTES ON BOOKS

THE primary published sources for the life of Bolívar are all in Spanish. O'Leary printed twenty-six volumes of documents, *Memorias* (Caracas, 1879–84), from which he compiled his *Bolívar y la Emancipación de Sur-América.* The first draft, in English, was never published; but it was translated into Spanish by his son and appeared in Caracas: volumes 1 and 2 in 1883 and volume 3 in 1915. A second edition in three volumes was printed in Madrid in 1915. The letters, *Cartas del Libertador*, ten volumes, were printed by Vicente Lecuna (Caracas, 1929–30) in a magnificent edition fully indexed. Three volumes of selected letters have been edited by R. Blanco-Fombona, 1913, 1921, and undated, and a selection in French, *Choix de Lettres, Discours et Proclamations*, has been published by the Institut International de Coopération Intellectuelle (Paris, 1934). Speeches and proclamations, *Discursos y Proclamaciones*, ed. R. Blanco-Fombona (Paris, 1913).

After O'Leary, the best life is that by Felipe Larrazábal, too partial to its subject but containing much valuable material: *Vida del Libertador Simón Bolívar*, Edición modernizada, prólogo y notas de R. Blanco-Fombona, two volumes (Madrid, 1918). Bolívar was attacked during his lifetime by the French adventurer, H. L. V. Ducoudray-Holstein, whose *Memoirs* appeared in English in 1830. An attack was also published by Colonel G. Hippisley (1819), who had gone out to serve under the Liberator in Venezuela, but was disappointed at not being promoted to the rank of general. The best and most balanced modern account is probably that given by J. Gil Fortoul in his *Historia Constitucional de Venezuela*, two volumes (Berlin, 1907–8; 2nd edition Caracas, 1930). Earlier lives in English include those by Clayton, *History of Simón Bolívar* (London, 1876), and F. Loraine Petre, *Simón Bolívar 'El Libertador'* (London, 1910); but important documents have become available since these books were published. More recent is H. Angell, *Simón Bolívar, South American Liberator* (New York, 1930); more novelesque biographies are those of Emil Ludwig, *Bolívar, the Life of an Idealist* (New York, 1942); Thomas Rourke, *Simón Bolívar* (New York and London, 1940), and Elizabeth Waugh, *Simón Bolívar* (London, 1944). Among the military histories is F. Rivas Vicuña, *Las Guerras de Bolívar, 1814–1817* (Caracas, 1922). For the early life of the Liberator may be recommended the sketch by C. F. Witzke, *Bosquejo de la vida de Simón Bolívar . . . hasta el Año de 1810*, published in the *Gaceta de los museos nacionales*, III, i–iii (Caracas, 1914), and the unfinished biography by Jules Mancini—which would have been the most complete in existence if it had not been interrupted by the author's death—*Bolívar et l'émancipation des colonies espagnoles, des origines à 1815* (Paris, 1912). Spanish translation (Paris, 1930). See also R. Blanco-Fombona, *La inteligencia de Bolívar*. Discurso de recepción, Acad. Nac. de la Hist. (Caracas, 1939). Among other recent French works is G. Lafond et

G. Tersane, *Bolívar et la libération de l'Amérique du Sud* (Paris, 1931). One of the most interesting contemporary accounts is the diary of Colonel Péroux de Lacroix, a French officer who served for a time on the Liberator's staff: *Diario de Bucaramanga,* publicado . . . por Cornelio Hispano (Paris, 1912). The portraits are studied by M. S. Sánchez in *Apuntes para la iconografía del Libertador* (Caracas, 1916). For general bibliography, R. A. Humphreys, *Latin America* (Chatham House Bibliographies; London, 1941).

Chapter One

The social and political history of South America in colonial times can be read in English and French. E. G. Bourne, *Spain in America, 1450–1580* (*The American Nation,* volume 3; New York and London, 1904) is still one of the best introductions to the age of discovery, and Arthur Helps, *The Spanish Conquest in America* (various editions), is still useful, particularly the edition by M. Oppenheim (New York, 1900). Mention must also be made of the *Histoire de l'expansion coloniale des peuples européens: Portugal et Espagne* (Brussels-Paris, 1907) by C. de Lannoy and H. van der Linden, and Leroy-Beaulieu, *De la colonization chez les peuples modernes,* sixth edition (Paris, 1908). For the vice-regal period the following books by Bernard Moses should be consulted: *The Spanish Dependencies in South America,* two volumes (London, 1914); *Spain's Declining Power in South America, 1730–1806* (University of California, 1919); *The Intellectual Background,* and *Spain Overseas* (Hispanic Society of America, 1929).

APPENDIX

The general history of the period is summarized by F. A. Kirkpatrick, *Latin America, a Brief History* (Cambridge, 1938); W. S. Robertson, *History of the Latin-American Nations*, second edition (New York, 1932), and *The Rise of the Spanish American Nations as told in the Lives of their Liberators* (New York, 1932); W. R. Shepherd, *Central and South America* (Home University Library, 1914); *The Republics of South America:* a report by a study-group of members of the Royal Institute of International Affairs (Oxford, 1937); J. F. Rippy, *Historic Evolution of Hispanic America* (Oxford, Blackwell, 1936); S. de Madariaga, *Cuadro histórico de las Indias: Introducción a Bolívar* (Buenos Aires, 1945).

Works on the Spanish empire, written from a modern standpoint, include S. Zavala, *New Viewpoints on the Spanish Colonization of America* (University of Pennsylvania, 1943); J. H. Parry, *The Spanish Theory of Empire in the 16th Century* (Cambridge, 1940); Fernando de los Ríos, *The Action of Spain in America*, in C. C. Griffin's *Concerning Latin American Culture* (New York, 1940), and his earlier study, *The Religious Character of Colonial Law in 16th-century Spain* (in *Proceedings* of the sixth International Congress of Philosophy, 1926); also Lewis Hanke, *The First Social Experiments in America* (Havard, 1935).

Some of the earlier writers, also, may be consulted with profit, e.g. Raynal, *Philosophical and Political History of the Settlements and Trade of the Europeans in the East and West Indies*, translated from the French (London, 1777); while the travellers at the end of the eighteenth century give a vivid picture of the world into which Bolívar was born: F. Depons, *Travels in South America . . . 1801 . . . and 1804, con-*

taining a Description of the Captain-generalship of Caracas, two volumes (London, 1807), and *A Voyage to the Eastern Part of Terra Firma, or the Spanish Main in South America* (New York, 1806); Woodbine Parish, *Buenos Ayres and the Provinces of the Rio de la Plata*, second edition (London, 1852). See also G. Desdevises du Dezert, *La société espagnole au XVIIIe Siècle*, second edition (in *Revue Hispanique*, New York-Paris, 1925), pp. 275–291, 331–340, 354–362, 546–559, etc.; P. Henríquez-Ureña, *Literary Currents in Hispanic America* (Harvard, 1945); and the very interesting works of Gilbert Chinard, *L'Exotisme américaine . . . au XVIe Siècle* (Paris, 1911)^e^ and *L'Amérique et le rêve exotique . . . au XVIIe et au XVIIIe Siècle* (Paris, 1913).

More closely related to Venezuela: J. Humbert, *Histoire de la Colombie et du Vénézuéla* (Paris, 1921), and *Les origines vénézuéliennes* (Bordeaux, 1905); Aristides Rojas, *Estudios históricos*, Serie 1 (Caracas, 1926), and *Lecturas históricas*, Serie 3 (Caracas, 1927); H. García Chuecos, *Estudios de historia colonial Venezolana*, two volumes (Caracas, 1937); J. B. Plaza, *Teresa Carreño* (Caracas, 1938); Marta Milinowski, *Teresa Carreño* (Yale, 1940), and *Music in Caracas during the Colonial Period* (1770–1811), in *Musical Quarterly* (New York, April, 1943). The fact that more books reached the Spanish colonies than has generally been supposed has been demonstrated by Irving A. Leonard (University of California Publications in Modern Philology, XVI, No. 3, 1933, and various articles in the *Hispanic Review*). See also *Latin America and the Enlightenment*: essays by Arthur P. Whitaker, Roland D. Hussey, and others (The Appleton-Century *Historical Essays*, New York and London, 1942).

APPENDIX

Chapter Two

See the biographies mentioned on pp. 269, 270, and the *Historia constitucional* of Gil Fortoul. The fullest account of Bolívar's tutor is given by Lozano y Lozano, *El maestro del Libertador* (Paris, 1914). For Rousseau, see *The Political Writings*, edited by C. E. Vaughan, two volumes (London, 1915), and for Rousseau in the Spanish-speaking world, various publications of J. R. Spell (*Hispanic Review*, and elsewhere). The *Memorias* of Servando Teresa de Mier have been edited by Alfonso Reyes (Madrid, 1917); his connexions with S. Robinson are brought out by Jean Sarrailh, *Enquêtes romantiques françaises-espagnoles* (Paris, 1933). Paris in 1804 is described in the *Mémoires* of Madame de Rémusat (II, 83 ff.), and in Henri d'Alméras, *La Vie parisienne sous le Consulat et l'Empire*, second edition (Paris, 1909). The complete text of Bolívar's impromptu declaration on the Aventine Hill is printed in *Homenaje al Libertador en su centenario* (Caracas, 1873), p. 72, and in J. D. Monsalve, *El ideal político del Libertador* (Madrid, 1916), pp. 28–30.

Chapter Three

In addition to the books already mentioned, C. Parra-Pérez, *Historia de la primera República de Venezuela*, two volumes (Caracas, 1939). For the visit of the French commissioners see W. H. Symth, *Life and Services of Capt. Philip Beaver* (London, 1829), pp. 173–177, and appendix 334–340. There is also *France and Latin American Independence* (Baltimore, 1939), by W. S. Robertson, whose important *Life of Miranda*, two volumes (Chapel Hill, 1929) should be consulted. C. W. Crawley discusses *French and English Influences in the Cortes of Cadiz, 1810–1811* (*Cambridge Historical Journal*, 1929, pp. 176–208). The *Memoirs of General Miller in the Service of the Republic of Peru*, two volumes, were published in London in 1828 (see volume II, p. 276).

Chapter Four

Sarmiento, *Facundo: Civilización y barbarie*, translated into English, *Life in the Argentine Republic in the Days of the Tyrants or Civilization and Barbarism* (New York, 1868), Part I, chapters 2 and 4. Bolívar's *Memoria de Cartagena* is printed by O'Leary. See comments in C. Parra-Pérez, *Bolívar*: *Contribución al estudio de sus ideas políticas* (Paris, 1928).

Chapter Five

The letter from Jamaica is printed by O'Leary, by Blanco-Fombona in *El pensamiento vivo de Bolívar* (Buenos Aires, 1942), and in *Antología del pensamiento de lengua española* (Mexico, 1945). For the life of Páez, see Cunninghame Graham, *José Antonio Páez* (London, 1929). The latest study of the British Legion is to be found in A. Hasbrouck, *Foreign Legionaries in the Liberation of Spanish America* (Columbia University Press, 1938). The *Address to the Venezuelan Congress at Angostura* has been printed by the Cambridge University Press (ed. F. A. Kirkpatrick, 1923); it is also printed with the Letter from Jamaica (see above). An English translation was included in *Colombia: being a Geographical . . . and Political Account of that Country* (London, 1822), vol. II, pp. 385–413.

For discussion and criticism see V. A. Belaunde, *Bolívar and the Political Thought of the Spanish American Revolution* (Baltimore, 1938). Also *Rousseau, the Political Writings*, ed. C. E. Vaughan, two volumes (London, 1915); Montesquieu, *De l'esprit des lois*, especially book IX, ch. 1, and book VIII, ch. 16; Henri Sée, *Idées politiques en France au XVIIIème Siècle* (Paris, 1925); *The Social and Political Ideas of Some Great Thinkers of the Age of Reason*, ed. F. J. G. Hearnshaw (London, 1930); Kingsley Martin, *French Liberal Thought in the 18th Century* (London, 1929). *The Federalist* has been reprinted in Everyman's Library, No. 519. Rocafuerte published his *Sistema colombiano* at Philadelphia (1823), and his *Cartas de un Americano sobre las ventajas de los gobiernos federativos* in London (1826). Bolívar, quoting from memory, attributed the saying on page 139 to Volney, but it is not to be found in any French or Spanish edition of his *Ruines ou méditations sur les révolutions des empires* (1791).

Chapter Six

Rómulo Gallegos, *Cantaclaro*; Hiram Bingham, *Journal of an Expedition across Venezuela and Colombia, 1906–7 . . . the Route of Bolívar's Celebrated March* (Newhaven, 1909).

Chapter Seven

The interview at Guayaquil has given rise to a large literature. A book giving the various sides to the question is *La entrevista de Guayaquil*, by E. de la Cruz, J. M. Goenaga, B. Mitre, and Carlos A. Villanueva (Madrid, 1914). E. de la Cruz's study is reprinted in *Bolívar por los más grandes escritores americanos* (Madrid, 1914). Carlos Villanueva has devoted a whole volume to the examination of the evidence: *Bolívar y el General San Martín*, in the series *La monarquía en América* (Paris, 1913). The evidence is summarized by "Cornelio Hispano" (Ignazio López) in *El Libro de Oro de Bolívar* (Paris, 1925). The case for San Martín is put forcibly by B. Mitre, *Historia de San Martín*, four volumes (Buenos Aires, 1890); there is a condensed translation by William Pilling, *The Emancipation of South America* (London, 1893); but these writers were without knowledge of essential documents. How San Martín struck an English contemporary may be read in the *Extracts from a Journal written on the Coasts of Chili, Peru, and Mexico, in the years 1820, 21, 22*, by Capt. Basil Hall (1824), 3rd ed., vol. I, pp. 212–315. The negotiations at Punchauca are described, in English, by V. A. Belaunde, *Bolívar and the Political Thought of the Spanish American Revolution* (Baltimore, 1938). In general, see the brief essay by Ricardo Levene, *El Americanismo de San Martín y Bolívar*, in *La Cultura histórica y el sentimiento de la nacionalidad* (Buenos Aires, 1942; Colección Austral, 303). Boundary questions are dealt with by Gordon Ireland, *Boundaries, Possessions and Conflicts in South America* (Harvard, 1938).

Chapters Eight and Nine

Bolívar's constitution for Bolivia is printed in *Antología del pensamiento de lengua española* (Mexico, 1945). For his political thought on this occasion, see the works of Belaunde and Parra-Pérez already mentioned. The literature on the Monroe Doctrine is extensive: see especially Dexter Perkins, *The Monroe Doctrine, 1823–1826* (Harvard, 1927). The policies of Castlereagh and Canning, and all the relevant documents, are examined by Sir Charles Webster, *Britain and the Independence of Latin America, 1812–1830*, two volumes (Oxford, 1938). Introduction published separately, 1944. An earlier account is found in Temperley, *The Foreign Policy of Canning* (in *The Cambridge History of British Foreign Policy*, volume II, ch. 2; 1923), and *The Foreign Policy of Canning, 1822–1827* (London, 1925). The relations with the U.S. are described by C. C. Griffin, *The U.S. and the Disruption of the Spanish Empire, 1810–1827* (Columbia University Press, 1937); the documents are printed by F. J. Urrutia, *Páginas de historia diplomática: Los Estados de América y las Repúblicas hispanoamericanas de 1810 a 1830* (Bogotá, 1917).

Chapters Ten and Eleven

The letter from Manuela Saenz was printed in the suppressed third volume of O'Leary's *Bolívar y la emancipación de Sur-América*, published in 1916. Garibaldi's *Memorie* have gone through various editions. The translation here follows the third (Florence, 1888); the passage is generally quoted incorrectly. For the *Diario de Bucaramanga*, see page 271. Developments since Bolívar's death are studied by Dr. R. A. Humphreys, *The Evolution of Modern Latin America* (Oxford, 1946).

Index

INDEX

INDEX

INDEX

INDEX

INDEX

INDEX

INDEX